N?W I KN!W MORE

THE REVEALING STORIES BEHIND EVEN MORE OF THE WORLD'S MOST INTERESTING FACTS

DAN LEWIS

AUTHOR OF *NOW I KNOW*

Adams Media

New York   London   Toronto   Sydney   New Delhi

DEDICATION

To Stephanie, Ethan, Alex, Annie, and my parents.

Adams Media
An Imprint of Simon & Schuster, Inc.
57 Littlefield Street
Avon, Massachusetts 02322

For information about special discounts for bulk purchases, please contact Simon & Schuster Special Sales at 1-866-506-1949 or business@simonandschuster.com.

The Simon & Schuster Speakers Bureau can bring authors to your live event. For more information or to book an event contact the Simon & Schuster Speakers Bureau at 1-866-248-3049 or visit our website at www.simonspeakers.com.

Interior illustrations © 123RF and Clipart.com

Now I Know title typography by Carla Rozman

Manufactured in the United States of America

10 9 8 7 6 5 4 3

Library of Congress Cataloging-in-Publication Data has been applied for.

ISBN 978-1-4405-8215-8
ISBN 978-1-4405-8216-5 (ebook)

CONTENTS

INTRODUCTION

I opened my first book, *Now I Know*, with a quote from Mark Twain that I think bears repeating, because it's still just as correct and now twice as relevant: "Truth is stranger than fiction, but it is because Fiction is obliged to stick to possibilities; Truth isn't."

The world is filled with stories that are literally incredible and unbelievable, shocking our sense of what's possible. Nonetheless, they're real. For more than four years, I've collected those stories—first as an ongoing e-mail newsletter; then as a book titled *Now I Know*, a precursor to this one; and now, in *Now I Know More*. You need not be familiar with either of this book's precedents, though. All you need to be is curious about the world and the unlikely things that history, science, technology, and life have thrown at us.

For example, have you ever seen a word in a dictionary and didn't think it was real? It may not have been. Or, doorknobs—everyone knows what they are, but why are they controversial . . . doubly so in Colorado? Of course, we all know that on 9/11, air traffic came to a halt. But how'd that happen, and what does it have to do with whales? For that matter, what does a home cleaning solution have to do with the War on Terror?

In the following stories and their bonus facts—each story has at least one bonus fact—we'll tackle all of that and more. We'll talk about the color pink, panda bears, shopping malls, birthdays, DNA, the post office, burritos, and a town that never existed. I've written these stories so that each one connects to the next in some way or another, because while I don't expect you to read this book in one sitting, I hope that each piece of mind-blowing trivia will encourage you to explore further. After all, curiosity is what got you here in the first place. When you're done with the book, don't worry—there's more. Every weekday, I send out a free e-mail newsletter with another one of these stories. You can get that at *http://NowIKnow.com*.

So let's begin. Let's steal the Empire State Building.

Really. That happened once. (Just go to the next page.)

STOLEN EMPIRE
HOW TO STEAL THE EMPIRE STATE BUILDING

$45 million, stolen.

It took a pair of incidents—one in December 2012 and another the following February—but seven people, all part of what the *New York Post* called "a sophisticated cyber crime ring" spanning the world, managed to get thousands of ATMs to wrongfully pay them a sum of money approaching the net worth of the *Boston Globe*. That's a huge heist. But it's tiny compared to one pulled off in Manhattan in late 2008. It took ninety minutes, and the property stolen was worth $2 billion. That's roughly the value of the Empire State Building.

Which makes sense, because that's exactly what was stolen.

Around Thanksgiving in 2008, a deed of sale came across a desk at New York City Hall, signifying the transfer of a building from Empire State Land Associates to a company called Nelots Properties. The description of the property conveyed by this deed of sale matched that of the Empire State Building, but the clerks who processed the paperwork either didn't notice or didn't care. All the important information was on the deed, as required, including the signatures of witnesses and that of the notary. The fact that one of the witnesses was named Fay Wray, the actress who played King Kong's captive as he ascended the Empire State Building in the 1933 film, likely escaped them. (To be fair, how many people in 2008 knew her name? It couldn't be all that many.) And that notary? He was a guy named Willie Sutton, who happened to share a name with a famous bank robber. Even the name of the acquiring company was a clue that something was awry; "Nelots," spelled backward, is "Stolen."

The good news for Empire State Land Associates is that Nelots was not a true threat to the rightful owners' property. Nelots didn't exist. It was a figment of the imagination of the *New York Daily News*, which concocted the fake deed of sale to demonstrate how easy it is to temporarily, and illegally, obtain "official" ownership of real estate.

As the *Daily News* noted, this stunt isn't just used by pranksters and jokesters. It's used by swindlers, and no, they aren't trying to move into your house—in fact, these con artists don't ever need to (and often don't) visit their newly but wrongly acquired property. These new "owners" can take out a mortgage or other line of credit against the property, and once they have the money in hand, disappear. The true owners are left with an unclear title, liens against their property, and at times, banks looking to foreclose even though the rightful owner never took out a loan. It's not only (or even mostly) the fault of the city clerk who processes the deeds. As a *Philadelphia City Paper* editor said in a video on deed fraud created by the University of Pennsylvania Law School, "It's pretty hard to stop a forged signature and a bribed notary. Where do you stop that? It's a little more difficult." The system doesn't make it all that difficult; in the same video, an attorney who has worked on these cases claimed, "It is easier to steal a home in the city of Philadelphia than it is to steal a purse." Given the *Daily News*'s ruse, this is probably true for New York, too, and probably many other places as well.

Homeowners and landlords aren't the only victims—the loans banks make often go unrepaid. Therefore many lending institutions have developed a system to alert them to potential fraud. The telltale sign: the mortgagee's failure to make his or her first payment, which one law enforcement agency describes as a "first payment default." The theory is simple: A true borrower would be able to pay the first bill, but one committing deed fraud would likely not be at the address and therefore never receive the bill, which would go unpaid.

As for the Empire State Building, the *Daily News* "returned" it before any of this was an issue.

BONUS FACT

It took nearly two decades before the Empire State Building turned a profit. Why? It couldn't attract tenants—it was much farther away from the two main train stations, Grand Central and Penn Station, than competing skyscrapers such as the Chrysler Building. The rental revenues were initially so poor that in its first year the Empire State Building earned as much revenue from its observation deck as it did from renters.

SAVED BY THE WIND
THE MOST UNLIKELY WAY TO SAVE A LIFE

Here's a crass joke: A man is at a dinner party in a fortieth-floor apartment. He announces to the rest, "You know, the wind out there is so strong that if you jump out the window, it will blow you all around the building and right back in!" The other guests laugh, but the man persists: "I'll prove it!" He jumps out the window and, sure enough, he floats around the building and re-enters safely through the same window. Another guest, wanting the thrill of a lifetime, quickly jumps out the window before anyone else can stop him—and plummets to his death.

The host glares at the first guest and says, "You can be a real jerk when you're drunk, Superman."

Again, that's a joke. But on December 2, 1979, Elvita Adams showed that sometimes, even everyday people can be a little bit super.

That evening, Adams, then age twenty-nine and living in the Bronx, decided to take her life. The reasons are unclear, but she had been in a fight with her landlord and was about to be evicted; she also suffered from depression. She went to the Empire State Building in midtown Manhattan to the observatory on the eighty-sixth floor, scaled a seven-foot fence (replete with steel spikes), and jumped.

That, in and of itself, is nothing terribly peculiar. A few dozen people have jumped to their deaths from the Empire State Building, the first occurring before the building was even completed when a laid-off worker took his life that way. In 1947, a twenty-three-year-old jumped, leaving a crossed-out suicide note about how an unnamed man would be "much better off without [her]" and that she would not have made a very good wife. Her body was found on a limousine at the building's base, and *LIFE* magazine ran a picture of her body, titling it, "The Most Beautiful Suicide." Just a few years ago, a fifty-four-year-old Manhattan woman ended her life in similar fashion.

But Adams did something almost none of the others had done: she survived. A wind gust—a very strong one—caught her and blew her back toward the building, albeit one floor down. She landed on a ledge, where a security guard found her before she could make another attempt. The only damage to her body? A fractured hip.

Adams was taken to a mental institution to recuperate. Her current whereabouts are not publicly known.

BONUS FACT

Suicide attempts at the Empire State Building are rare, but the same unfortunately cannot be said about the Golden Gate Bridge in San Francisco, the most popular such site in the United States. (The Nanjing Yangtze River Bridge in China is widely regarded as the world's most popular suicide bridge, and the Golden Gate Bridge is number two.) We don't know, officially, how many people have taken their lives there because when the number hit 997, authorities stopped counting to avoid giving anyone the incentive of being jumper number 1,000. Whatever the number is, it could have been much higher. In 1994, California Highway Patrol Sergeant Kevin Briggs was assigned to patrol the bridge. Since then, he's managed to talk an estimated 200 people out of jumping.

BUMMER AND LAZARUS
SAN FRANCISCO'S UNLIKELY ROYALTY

Henry Rippey, a local drunk, was in jail. His crime was taking the life of another, known only as Bummer. When word of this reached his cellmate, David Popley, the latter extracted some vigilante justice. Popley punched Rippey in the nose.

Inmate-on-inmate violence is, unfortunately, not all that rare, making the punch a nonstory. The fact that this happened in San Francisco in 1865 doesn't add much to it either. Add that Rippey's murder weapon was his shoe—he kicked Bummer to death—and maybe we're getting a little closer . . . but not really. Even the fact that Mark Twain wrote Bummer's obituary doesn't make Popley's defense of the victim's honor all that unique.

But here's the thing: Bummer was a dog.

And yes, Mark Twain really did write his obituary.

Dogs weren't always domesticated in California in the 1860s. Around that time both Los Angeles and San Francisco had problems with "free-ranging" dogs—ferals and strays—running amok and often outnumbering people. Dogcatchers were common municipal authorities, and when a dogcatcher nabbed himself a stray, the dog was put to sleep with poison. But one ability could save a stray pup from death—ferreting out and killing rats.

By all accounts, Bummer was a great ratter, but his rise to fame came when, in 1861, another dog found himself on the losing side of a battle with a third, larger dog. Bummer came to the smaller dog's aid and rescued him from the skirmish. Afterward, Bummer brought the smaller dog food and kept him warm. The second dog, later named Lazarus, survived, and for the rest of his life, he was Bummer's sidekick. As a team, the two were even more efficient at catching rats; one source reports that they once nabbed eighty-five rodents in roughly twenty minutes.

Their reputations made them local heroes. When Lazarus was caught by a new dogcatcher in 1862, a groundswell of public support resulted in his release and the pair's exemption from anti-stray ordinances. Legend has it that, a week later, they helped stop a runaway horse, which was dragging a cart through downtown San Francisco.

Lazarus passed away in 1863, and the *San Francisco Chronicle* published a lengthy obituary in his memory. Two years later, the previously mentioned Mr. Rippey caused the death of Bummer when he kicked the dog in a drunken stupor. The city arrested Rippey after the public demanded justice for the area's unofficial mascot and über-pet.

BONUS FACT

Bummer and Lazarus's legacy has rubbed off on a San Francisco–area company you may have heard of: Google. Google's corporate code of conduct contains a "dog policy," which reads, "Google's affection for our canine friends is an integral facet of our corporate culture. We like cats, but we're a dog company, so as a general rule we feel cats visiting our offices would be fairly stressed out."

THE EMPEROR
THE MAN WHO RECEIVED A FUNERAL FIT FOR A KING

On January 8, 1880, Emperor Norton I collapsed on his way to a lecture at a local university. He died before help could arrive. His death made front-page news in the largest newspaper of the area, under the headline "Le Roi Est Mort" (The King Is Dead). A similar headline was splashed across the second-largest newspaper of the locale. At his funeral two days later, thousands—perhaps as many as 30,000, despite the city's population being only about 200,000—came to pay their respects. The newspaper reported the next day that within hours, the line of mourners was out the door, hundreds of people long.

But his empire wasn't real. Joshua Abraham Norton—or his Imperial Majesty, Norton I, Emperor of the United States and Protector of Mexico—was a delusional (or at least, eccentric) pauper with a flair for grandeur. And the city of San Francisco seemed to love him for it.

The United States, of course, has never had an emperor, let alone one who was also the Protector of Mexico (the Monroe Doctrine notwithstanding). That mattered little to Norton. Born in England in the early 1800s, he inherited a large sum of money upon his father's death and moved from South Africa to San Francisco in 1849. Over the next few years, he successfully invested in real estate in the area and was worth a reported $250,000 in the 1850s—the equivalent of well over $6 million today. But he would soon lose his fortune. A famine in China led to rice shortages in San Francisco, and a rapid increase in prices looked as if it was on the horizon. Norton started buying up rice coming in from Peru at twelve and a half cents a pound, expecting to corner the market, but other shipments from Peru made it to the city—and the price fell to about three cents a pound. Norton lost money not only on the transaction but also on litigation to try and void his contract. In 1858, he left San Francisco, bankrupt.

He returned to the city at some point in 1859, but he was no longer interested in the rice or real estate businesses. Instead, Norton fancied himself as some strange kind of political activist, and on September 17, 1859, he sent a letter to various area newspapers proclaiming himself Norton I, Emperor of the United States. At first, the newspapers took it as a strange joke from a formerly well-known well-to-do citizen, but it soon became clear that Norton had lost more than his riches when the rice deal went bad. In October, the self-crowned emperor issued his first decree, abolishing Congress. (When Congress did not vacate, Emperor Norton ordered the army "to procede [*sic*] with a suitable force to clear the Halls of Congress.") He also instituted what may be the world's first swear jar, when he called for a $25 fine for anyone who used a certain F-word—"Frisco."

Despite his apparent madness, Norton was eminently likable and well received by the community. A local army post gave him a uniform befitting a commander of a real army, not just the one in his own head. Norton, being a sovereign, issued his own currency, and local citizens and businesses used it in day-to-day transactions.

Norton is buried in Colma, California. His gravestone memorializes him as "Norton I, Emperor of the United States and Protector of Mexico," just as he lived.

BONUS FACT

Norton I isn't the only person buried in Colma, California—also buried there are Joe DiMaggio, William Randolph Hearst, Wyatt Earp, and Levi Strauss. The town, founded in 1924 (Norton's remains were moved there in 1934), was designed to be a necropolis; it is made up mostly of cemeteries or land designated as future cemeteries. The residents of the town take their role in life (and death) with humor. In 2006, the mayor of Colma told the *New York Times* that the city "has 1,500 above-ground residents and 1.5 million underground," while the town's official website motto is, "It's Great to Be Alive in Colma."

THE ODYSSEY
THE MOVE THAT SAVED A CITY

"A City on the Move."

That's the motto of the town of Ulysses, Kansas, which has about 6,000 residents. It's named after Ulysses S. Grant, the eighteenth president of the United States (not the Homeric hero). It's the largest municipality in Grant County (also named for the president) and is home to about 75 percent of the county's residents.

And that motto is to be taken literally.

Ulysses was founded in 1885 and, according to newspaper reports from that era, was well situated for growth. Not only did it sit on the east-west rail line of the time, but unlike many surrounding areas, the water table was only about thirty feet down, allowing for relatively easy access to fresh well water. (Many other areas required wells a few hundred feet deep.) By 1889, the town had a large schoolhouse, four hotels, twelve restaurants and another dozen saloons, six gambling halls, and an opera house. Nearly 1,500 people had moved to Ulysses.

Then the droughts came, turning this once-thriving boomtown, colloquially, to dust. By 1906, the town's population hovered around 100—a far cry from its peak nearly two decades prior.

To make matters worse, the boom years of the mid-1880s were partially financed through a public debt offering. To meet the infrastructure needs of this growing city, town leaders issued municipal bonds, amassing well over $80,000 in debt. (Accounting for inflation, that's the modern-day equivalent of more than $2 million.) As was probably common for that era, the town's leadership didn't use that money to dig more wells (which might have staved off a drought) or other such improvements. Instead, they pocketed the money and never paid down the debt. Bondholders were less than pleased, and the next generation of Ulysses residents paid for their predecessors' sins via sky-high property (per one report, a 600 percent levy) and residency taxes.

Often, when things like that happen—when taxes get too high—residents move. That's kind of what occurred in this case. But there's a big difference: the people took the town with them.

Toward the end of 1908, Ulysses's remaining townsfolk purchased a new area of land about two miles west of Ulysses itself. In February 1909, the people started to move. Buildings were placed on horse-drawn skids and wagons and pulled to the new location of Ulysses. One of the hotels was cut into two parts and, over the course of several days, transported to the new site. By June of that same year, all the residents had moved, as had many of the municipal buildings, and the old town of Ulysses became a bondholder-owned ghost town.

BONUS FACT

Ulysses S. Grant was born Hiram Ulysses Grant. When he was nominated to attend West Point, the nominating congressman accidentally wrote his name wrong. Grant adopted the incorrect name, likely hoping to avoid confusion at the academy (and not, as some sources suggest, because his birth name bore the initials "HUG"). The middle initial, therefore, doesn't stand for anything, but as his mother's maiden name was Simpson, many sources assert that is Grant's middle name.

GENERAL ORDER NUMBER ELEVEN
WHEN JEWS WERE BARRED FROM AMERICA

General Order Number Eleven was short. Three items were wrapped into one edict. It read:

1. "The Jews, as a class violating every regulation of trade established by the Treasury Department and also department orders, are hereby expelled from the Department within twenty-four hours from the receipt of this order.
2. "Post commanders will see to it that all of this class of people be furnished passes and required to leave, and anyone returning after such notification will be arrested and held in confinement until an opportunity occurs of sending them out as prisoners, unless furnished with permit from headquarters.
3. "No passes will be given these people to visit headquarters for the purpose of making personal application of trade permits."

In short, "no Jews allowed," effective nearly immediately.

But the "Department" wasn't a section of Nazi-controlled Europe or Inquisition-era Spain. The edict wasn't issued by Adolf Hitler. It was issued by Ulysses S. Grant, who would later be president of the United States. The year was 1862, and the "Department" was the "Department of Tennessee," an area consisting of western Tennessee, western Kentucky, and northern Mississippi.

In the spring of 1862, Grant, then a general of the Union army, made great advances in the American Civil War, taking control of many of the areas listed previously. His next goal was to march south, with Vicksburg, Mississippi, in his sights. But commanding the army wasn't his only job. Despite the war, the North and South continued to have some limited economic activity between them; the North bought cotton from Southern plantations. Grant was also charged with enforcing the Union-set limits on the amount of cotton that could legally be imported into the North. Illegal cotton dealings were rampant and legal ones were a bother; merchants would come to Grant's headquarters seeking permits, as one historian noted. Grant viewed most of these merchants as war profiteers, and on December 17, he decided to ban them from the region by proclamation. But for some reason—*Slate* notes that most of the "smugglers and traders [. . .] were not Jewish at all"—Grant's order targeted Jews, and all Jews in the area, for that matter.

The order was of limited effectiveness (against Jews, that is; it was almost entirely ineffective against smugglers because most weren't subject to the order) for two reasons. First, the order didn't get distributed immediately, as communications lines were disrupted by Confederate raids just hours later (unrelated to the order, though). Second, word of the order spread throughout the country and eventually to President Lincoln, who ordered Grant to rescind it. He did so, officially, on January 18 of the following year. Many Jews in the area were indeed displaced during the month the order was in force, however, and it kindled fears of anti-Semitism throughout the country. As *Slate* further said, "It brought to the surface deep-seated fears that, in the wake of the Emancipation Proclamation, Jews might replace blacks as the nation's most despised minority." Further, for perhaps the first time, American

Jews needed to openly consider whether to vote for candidates who were good for the country but bad for Jews themselves.

Grant, for his part, claimed he had not intended the anti-Semitic aspects of the order. His headquarters showed some surprise when Jews who were not smugglers were relocated, even though the plain language of the order included all Jews. Grant also later stated that he didn't draft the order and hastily signed it without reviewing it, but other communications by Grant around that period also singled out "Jews" or "Israelites." To his credit, though, during his term in the Oval Office, Grant became the first U.S. president to attend a synagogue service.

BONUS FACT

The synagogue Grant visited, Adas Israel Congregation in Washington, DC, has two other historical firsts in its history. According to its website, it was the first synagogue in the United States to be addressed by both Dr. Martin Luther King Jr. and the Dalai Lama.

INKOSHERATION
WHEN DIETARY LAWS AND PRISON DON'T MIX

Depending on one's definition, there are roughly 5 to 10 million Jews living in the United States, constituting about 2.5 percent of the population. A smaller sub-group—perhaps as many as a million—keeps kosher, which means they follow a set of religious dietary restrictions to some degree or another. With many different customs and interpretations of the law, the rules about what's kosher and what's not are complicated—too complicated to detail in these pages. However, there are a few things that most agree upon: You can't eat pork or shellfish, and there's no mixing milk and meat (sorry, no cheeseburgers). And the whole idea that a rabbi has to bless the food? That's a myth.

In general, the food is supposed to be supervised. The rabbi watches its preparation and the processes involved to ensure that nothing disallowed happens. When the food is shipped after preparation, it is typically sealed so that the end consumer knows that nothing has been introduced since. That's why kosher airplane food, you may have noticed, is served in foil or plastic wrap, while typical in-flight meals are served already open.

It also may be why kosher meals are unusually popular in prison.

In the spring of 2013, the *Jewish Daily Forward* noted that an estimated 24,000 inmates ate kosher foods in American prisons, but only 4,000 considered themselves Jewish before their incarceration. The *New York Times* published an article in early 2014 suggesting that nearly 5,000 inmates in Florida alone requested kosher meals, with only a fraction having claimed to be Jewish prior to that request. Kosher meals, when in prison, aren't just for those who subscribe to certain religious beliefs.

Media reports suggest that the reason ostensibly non-Jewish prisoners prefer the alternative menu isn't only because of taste. Some feel the fact that the meals are pre-prepared and wrapped makes them safer to eat. As one prison chaplain told the *Times*, inmates are often concerned (rationally or otherwise) "about how the food could be adulterated, how the prison uses out-of-date products, how they use things that don't meet U.S.D.A. standards, how sex offenders may be handling their food." Pre-packaged, sealed meals make all of that less likely.

It also makes the meals tradable commodities. Citing the practice at one Californian prison, the *Forward* notes that "prisoners who keep kosher receive three daily meals in a sack that they bring back to their cells. [. . .] Inmates frequently trade kosher food for prison-issued paper money, which can be used to buy items in the facility's canteen." Kosher food, in an ironic twist, fuels the black market for contraband items.

Unfortunately for taxpayers, the kosher food isn't cheap, costing two to three times that of non-kosher meals. While some states try to identify opportunists, it's hard to do so. After all, and for good reason, American laws and culture generally allow people to be part of whatever religion they want, without any second-guessing by the government.

BONUS FACT

Ever notice a circled "U" on your food packages? That's one of many symbols that certify the food is kosher. In that case, the certifying organization is the Orthodox Union, or "OU" for short—the circle around the "U" is actually an "O." If you see a "D" next to the circled "U," that means from a kosher certification standpoint, the food item is dairy, which, as noted previously, kosher-keeping Jews do not combine with meat.

TEXAS'S LAST LAST MEAL
WHY DEATH ROW INMATES IN TEXAS DON'T GET TO PICK THEIR LAST MEALS

On June 7, 1998, a forty-nine-year-old African-American man from Texas, named James Byrd Jr., was brutally murdered by three men. While Byrd was still alive, the perpetrators tied his ankles to the back of a pickup truck and dragged him for three miles; Byrd was decapitated in the process. Byrd's murder resulted in legislation, both on the state and federal level, that addresses criminal activities typically called "hate crimes." Two of Byrd's three assailants were sentenced to death, with the third sentenced to life in prison without possibility of parole. Of the two given the death penalty, one still sits on Death Row. The other, Lawrence Russell Brewer, was executed by the state of Texas on September 21, 2011.

Brewer's ritual "last meal" was Texas's last such "last meal."

The origin of the traditional "last meal" of the condemned person's choosing—a final rite of passage before the inmate's final passing—has been lost to antiquity. But most U.S. states with the death penalty still allow those about to be executed a special meal beforehand (albeit not always as their true "last" meal). Texas, until Brewer, was no exception. Some requests were basic but high-end, with at least two men (Ronald Clark O'Bryan in 1984 and

Dennis Bagwell in 2005) asking for, and receiving, feasts with steak and french fries. Other requests were just plain strange. In 2001, a murderer named Gerald Lee Mitchell requested that the state give him a bag of assorted Jolly Ranchers as a last meal; this request was granted. In 2000, a man named Odell Barnes asked for "justice, equality, and world peace." In 1990, James Edward Smith requested a lump of dirt used for voodoo rituals, as a way of marking his body for the afterlife. His request was denied, and he was given a cup of yogurt instead.

Brewer's request? Per the *New York Times*, he asked for:

two chicken-fried steaks with gravy and sliced onions; a triple-patty bacon cheeseburger; a cheese omelet with ground beef, tomatoes, onions, bell peppers and jalapeños; a bowl of fried okra with ketchup; one pound of barbecued meat with half a loaf of white bread; three fajitas; a meat-lover's pizza; one pint of Blue Bell Ice Cream; a slab of peanut-butter fudge with crushed peanuts; and three root beers.

The state provided him with this meal, costing hundreds of dollars and consisting of thousands of calories. Brewer, claiming he was not very hungry, ate exactly none of it.

The next day, state legislators asked the Department of Criminal Justice to end the tradition of "last meals." One lawmaker stated, "It is extremely inappropriate to give a person sentenced to death such a privilege. It's a privilege which the perpetrator did not provide to their victim." The Department of Criminal Justice chairperson agreed, and the tradition ended. Since then, per the *Houston Chronicle*, "Last meals will consist of whatever is on the menu for all prisoners"—with no special adjustments for those about to be executed.

BONUS FACT

In 2007, Tennessee executed a man named Philip Workman. For his last meal, Workman requested that a vegetarian pizza be donated to a homeless person (no one specifically), but prison officials, per CNN, denied that request, telling the news agency that "they do not donate to charities." Nevertheless, Workman's last wishes were carried out many times over by others. According to the same CNN article, donors from around the country rose to the occasion, donating hundreds of pizzas to Nashville-area homeless shelters.

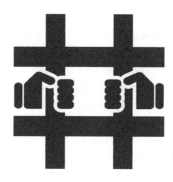

PRISON PINK
THE COLOR OF CALM

In the 1960s, a Swiss psychotherapist named Max Lüscher developed what is now known as the Lüscher color test, a system to help describe someone's personality. Dr. Lüscher would give the person eight cards, each of a different color—blue, yellow, red, green, violet, brown, grey, and black—and ask the subject to put them in order from most preferred to least preferred. Figuring that our taste in colors was something created by our subconscious selves, Dr. Lüscher further surmised that people of similar personality types would rank colors similarly.

The Lüscher color test is not often used anymore, since its validity has been widely questioned and its results do not match up well with better-received personality tests. However, Dr. Lüscher's work ushered in other research into the role color plays in our psyches.

Which is why it may be a good idea to paint prison cells pink.

In the 1970s, Alexander Schauss, a scientist in Tacoma, Washington, began exploring whether seeing a certain color could cause our emotional states to change. After a series of tests, he concluded that a certain shade of pink—#FF91AF if you're a web developer, CMYK 0-43-41-0 if print is more your thing—has a calming effect, taking the edge off of those who are overly aggressive. Specifically, Schauss noted that this shade of pink caused a measurable physiological reaction; there was "a marked effect on lowering the heart rate, pulse, and respiration as compared to other colors."

In early 1979 a local naval prison put Schauss's finding into action. The experiment was a simple one. The naval officers painted the walls of an 18' x 24' cell a bubblegum-like, Pepto Bismol–ish shade of pink recommended by Schauss. Some inmates were confined in the cell for a short time, as inmates would typically be in any prison cell. According to the follow-up report, the experiment worked: not only were there "no incidents of erratic or hostile behavior during the initial phase of confinement," but the navy reported that even fifteen minutes of exposure to the pink-walled room resulted in a noticeable reduction in aggressive behavior after release from the cell. Schauss, as reported by *USA Today*, claimed that before the introduction of the pink cell, the naval correctional center averaged one assault on staff per day. After? Only one such assault over the next six months.

Schauss named the color Baker-Miller Pink, after the directors of the naval correctional institute who agreed to test his theory. Others have called it "Drunk Tank Pink" after the colloquial name for small jail cells, and it's not uncommon to see jails and prisons with pink walls for these purposes. But one other place has given it a different name—and a different use. If you go to the University of Iowa's Kinnick Stadium, you'll find the walls, lockers, and even the urinals of the visiting football team's locker room painted Baker-Miller Pink, an explicit attempt to make the opposing team less aggressive when they take to the football field.

BONUS FACT

In 2010, the use of pink resulted in a lawsuit against a prison in South Carolina. But it wasn't the walls that were colored pink—it was the uniforms of those who, while in prison, engaged in some sort of sexual misconduct. The prison wanted to use this tactic as a punishment, embarrassing inmates in front of their peers, but the lawsuit against the prison claimed that the pink uniforms made the inmates the target of assaults.

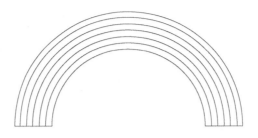

THE CASE OF THE MISSING MAGENTA
WHY YOU CAN'T SEE PINK (EVEN THOUGH YOU CAN)

Roy G. Biv.

That's not a person. It's a mnemonic device for remembering the colors in the visible spectrum of light, or in another sense, the colors of rainbows. Red, Orange, Yellow, Green, Blue, Indigo, and Violet. In between each of these colors is almost every other color we can detect . . . "almost" being the operative word.

The exception? Magenta. Go find a picture of a rainbow and you'll notice that magenta (often called pink), just isn't there. But, color-blindness aside, we can clearly see it. What's going on here?

First, let's talk about rainbows. Light comes in all sorts of wavelengths, and we humans can detect light in many of those wavelengths. (We can't see all of them—infrared and ultraviolet are two of the more commonly known invisible ones, but radio waves, x-rays, and gamma rays are also examples.) The light itself doesn't actually have a color—as Isaac Newton observed, "The rays, to speak properly, are not colored. In them there is nothing else than a certain power and disposition to stir up a sensation of this or that color." Our brains just associate different wavelengths with different colors. The range of 380 nanometers to about 450 nanometers are seen as various shades of violet, for example. Magenta, though, doesn't have an associated wavelength.

Instead, our brain just kind of makes it up when other information comes in.

Our eyes have photoreceptor cells called rods and cones. Rods detect the presence and amount of light, even if there are only small amounts, but cannot help us determine the color of things. Cones, which require more light before they turn on, help us figure out the colors. (That's why when it's dark, we often can't tell what color things are.) Humans typically have three types of cones: red, blue, and green. Everything the cones detect, therefore, is actually just one of those three colors, and our brains fill in the gaps so we can "see" the other colors of the rainbow. When a yellow wavelength comes in, for example, the red and green cones are triggered. Our brains interpret that as "yellow," and bananas, school buses, and lemons are better off for it. This makes sense . . . just ask Roy G. Biv. If you look between red and green, you'll see yellow is situated right in there.

Magenta occurs when the red and blue cones are stimulated. That's a problem if you look at the rainbow, because there's no "between" red and blue, as the ends of the spectrum don't connect with each other. The brain needs to do something with that information, and magenta seems like a pretty good solution, although for no obvious reason. After all, as *Scientific American* said (echoing Newton's observation), color "is all in your head [. . .]. It is a sensation that arises in your brain." If we're going to make up the colors anyway, there's no reason to limit ourselves to the stuff found in the visible spectrum—and the result is pink.

BONUS FACT

As noted earlier, when our eyes detect yellow wavelengths, that light is captured by the red and green cones and translated into what we think of as yellow. Most computer monitors (and TV and smartphone screens, for that matter) take advantage of this conversion process and skip the first step—there's no yellow wavelengths being used whatsoever. (That's also true for cyan, brown, and of course, magenta.) All the colors the monitors show are actually just a mix of red, blue, and green light. If you could magnify your screen a lot, you'd see a series of red, blue, and green dots, and that's it—there are only three colors there.

THE CRAYON MAN'S SECRET
THE SHOCKING TRUTH BEHIND
THE MAN OF MANY COLORS

In 1903, the husband and wife team of Edwin and Alice Binney created the first wax crayon. Mr. Binney and his cousin, C. Harold Smith, owned a colorant company called the Binney and Smith Company, which, on July 10 of that year, introduced the couple's new product—Crayola crayons. In the century-plus since, the company (now officially the Crayola company) has introduced more than 400 different colors of crayons, of which 133 are considered "standard" colors available in their pack of 120. (Crayola has retired thirteen colors over the years, including Blue Gray in 1990 and Thistle in 2000.) In recent years, Crayola produces 3 billion crayons each year, and over its history it has produced well over 100 billion crayons.

Emerson Moser was one of the people responsible for many of those crayons. He was a Crayola employee working as a crayon molder—a person who pours the molten wax into the molds, shaping it into the recognizable (and useful) crayon shapes as it dries. For more than thirty years, day in and day out, Moser made crayons. Roughly 100 times a day, he'd pour wax into molds designed for 2,400 crayons. Over the course of his career, he molded an estimated 1.4 billion crayons. Periwinkle or Peach, Burnt Sienna or Burnt Umber, it didn't matter the color.

That last part—that the color didn't matter—that's pretty important. Because when he retired, Emerson Moser admitted he was colorblind.

The infirmity was, of course, something you'd normally not want from a man whose job it was to make one of ten dozen different colors. However, Moser's colorblindness, he'd later explain to the Associated Press, was slight; his biggest problem was determining the difference between similar shades of blues and greens. (That's probably not all that strange—can many of us really tell the difference between Aquamarine and Turquoise Blue, or between Jungle Green and Fern, for example?) He told reporters that he found out he was colorblind in 1953, when a doctor discovered the issue during a routine physical exam, but "it was so slight that if the doctor wouldn't have tested me, I probably would have never noticed it."

His job didn't involve making sure that the right labels were on the right crayons, anyway—the crayons, after hardening in the molds, went to another area for that part of the manufacturing process. That being the case, the company was okay with the odd little fact that their most senior crayon molder wasn't able to differentiate between all 120 colors. Besides, Moser was a top employee: as of his retirement in 1990, Moser's record of 1.4 billion crayons molded stood above anyone else in the company.

BONUS FACT

In 1962, Crayola introduced Peach as one of the colors in its forty-eight-pack. It wasn't a new color, though. The color was originally introduced in 1949 under the name "Flesh," even though not all children have peach-colored skin tones.

DOUBLE BONUS

On February 6, 1996, Crayola molded its 100 billionth crayon, officially speaking. (It's an estimate—there's no reason to believe that Crayola kept an accurate count.) To celebrate, the company had a special molder come in to make the historic crayon. Not Emerson Moser, though—that honor went to Fred Rogers, better known from *Mr. Rogers' Neighborhood*.

INVISIBLE PINK
THE UNLIKELY COLOR OF CAMOUFLAGE

The Supermarine Spitfire was a small aircraft used by the British Royal Air Force in World War II for recon purposes, flying at low altitudes. Typically, Spitfires came with dark colors such as green on top. If an enemy plane were to pass overhead, the green-painted Spitfire would blend in with the terrain below.

But not all of them were green. Some were painted pink.

World War II took place well before the era of spy satellites, drones, and other technological advances that make overhead intel much easier to gather. For the British to know what the Germans were up to, they needed to fly overhead and, literally, take pictures. Many in the Royal Air Force (RAF) were tasked with photo reconnaissance missions, and the Spitfire—a small, one-man fighter—was one of the few planes able to penetrate (or evade) the Germans' outer defenses. But getting past the perimeter was only the first step toward the ultimate goal. The Spitfire still needed to fly over the targeted areas, take its pictures, and return safely. That required evading detection for much longer, ideally for the entire mission.

The RAF allowed photo recon units to experiment a bit with how to get that part done, especially when it came to painting the planes. Over the course of the war, the Spitfires were outfitted in all sorts of colors. Green made sense when in aerial combat while pink obviously did not—against the green backdrop of the ground or ocean below, the Spitfires would be nearly instantly noticed. But when on recon missions, the backdrops were the skies.

So the theory the RAF employed? Paint the planes pink and use the sunsets, sunrises, and most importantly, the clouds as your allies.

As the website *http://io9.com* explained, the cloud layer proved to be excellent cover for these planes. The Spitfires would run their missions at a relatively low altitude, hanging as close to the bottom of the clouds as possible. Enemy planes would have trouble seeing them through or against clouds, as would forces on the ground. The pink planes, which stood out on the ground, were much harder to detect when in the air—which is where they were performing their mission.

Very little is known about these planes—the number painted pink, how frequently they were used, etc. (Given that they were on spy missions, that seems reasonable.) We do know they had a meaningful impact in the outcome of World War II. Many of the photos of pink Spitfires show them decorated with black-and-white stripes on the rear part of the plane. Those stripes were added after D-Day, signifying that the plane was used in support of the successful invasion.

BONUS FACT

Planes weren't the only things turned "invisible pink" during the war. The Supreme Allied Commander South East Command, Louis Mountbatten, noticed that a ship still in pre-war lavender appeared to vanish against the horizon at dawn and dusk. Believing that this would give the Royal Navy an advantage, Mountbatten ordered that several ships be painted in a dark pink approaching grey, now called Mountbatten Pink. Other naval officers had their ships painted that color, starting a trend. Whether the color provided any actual camouflage value is unknown—it was never tested in any scientific manner.

TRIPLE PLAY
THE WORLD WAR II BASEBALL GAME WITH TWO LOSERS

Collectively, Baseball Hall of Fame managers Joe McCarthy and Leo Durocher were at the helms of their respective teams for forty-eight seasons, winning well over 4,000 games. Their managerial careers overlapped in the late 1930s and through the 1940s. At times they were cross-town rivals—from 1939 until 1946, McCarthy managed the New York Yankees while Durocher was the skipper for the still-in-Brooklyn Dodgers. Even though there was no interleague play back then, at least twice, the two commanded their teams from the same ballpark. Many baseball fans know about one of them, as McCarthy's Yankees beat Durocher's Dodgers in the 1941 World Series. The other one, though, was a special case. Not only were the Yankees and Dodgers in the same stadium, but they were in the same dugout.

That's because they were both the visiting team. The game was held neither at Yankee Stadium nor at the Dodgers' home turf of Ebbets Field. The teams were at the Polo Grounds, home of the New York Giants. The Giants themselves were there too. They were in the home dugout, and all three teams were playing against each other in one of the strangest games in baseball history.

The date was June 26, 1944. That might seem like a perfectly normal day for a perfectly normal baseball game, but the year changed things. The United States and much of the Western world was caught in the throes of World War II. War is expensive, and just about everyone was doing what they could to support the war effort. New York's sportswriters were no exception. As a scholar writing for the Society for American Baseball Research (SABR) discovered, a group of sportswriters had an idea for a "three-sided" game—one that's never happened since.

The rules were simple: It was a nine-inning baseball game, but instead of teams alternating their time in the field or at bat, they rotated. In the top of the first, the Dodgers came to bat against the Yankees, and in the bottom of the first, the teams switched sides. Then the Dodgers came back up to the plate for the top of the second. So far, normal. But the team pitching to them now wasn't the Yankees. It was the Giants. The two NL rivals faced off for that inning, and in the third, the Dodgers took a breather in the shared away-team dugout while the Yankees and Giants faced off. This pattern repeated twice over the next six innings.

The Dodgers won the game, with five runs to the Yankees' one and the Giants' zero. But the real winner of this exhibition was the War Bonds effort—the more than 50,000 people attending the three-way contest purchased an estimated $6.5 million of them during the course of the game.

BONUS FACT

An unassisted triple play occurs when all three outs in an inning are recorded in one play by the same fielder. It's one of the rarest events in baseball. As of the 2013 Major League Baseball season, there have been only fifteen unassisted triple plays in the league's history. That's rarer than a pitcher throwing a perfect game (twenty-one times since 1900) or a batter slugging four home runs in a game (sixteen times).

CHECKMATE
WHAT NOT TO DO WITH A CHECK FOR A MILLION DOLLARS

In the baseball world, a team's leadoff hitter has a specific role: get on base and, ultimately, get into a position to score a run. If you ask a baseball fan who is the greatest leadoff hitter of all time, he or she will almost certainly say, "Rickey Henderson." Henderson, the career leader in both runs scored and stolen bases, was well known for wreaking havoc on pitchers while he was on the base paths.

He also managed to wreak havoc on the Oakland Athletics' finance department.

Henderson made his Major League debut as a member of the A's (as the Athletics have become known) midway through the 1979 season. For the next ten years, he'd play for both the A's and Yankees and was easily the league's biggest base-stealing threat—he led the league in the category in nine of the ten seasons.

Before the 1990 season, Henderson became a free agent for the first time. While the "Man of Steal" had already earned more than $10 million over his career to that point, Rickey (as he'd refer to himself) was about to get a much larger payday from the A's—a four-year contract guaranteeing roughly $12 million in salary. Of that $12 million,

$1 million was due up front in the form of a signing bonus. The A's paid him by check.

The novelty of a million-dollar check was not lost on Henderson.

After the 1990 season, the A's finance department tried to balance the books, only to find a $1 million overage—they had too much money in the bank, given what they thought they had paid out. An inquest showed the likely culprit: for some reason, the million-dollar check made out to Henderson had never cleared. The A's called up Rickey and asked if he knew what had happened, and luckily for the finance people, he did.

Henderson never cashed the check. Instead, he had it framed and hung it on one of his walls. The check, as Henderson would later explain, was a constant reminder that he had made it—that he was a millionaire—and he wanted it to be in a place where he'd see it every day.

The A's asked him to make a copy of the check, frame that copy, and deposit the actual one. Henderson, fortunately, agreed.

BONUS FACT

There are a lot of really great Henderson stories on the Internet, with varying degrees of truth. For example, despite what some websites say, he never asked a teammate how long it takes to drive to the island nation of the Dominican Republic. But Rickey did once fall asleep on an ice pack, getting frostbite in the process—a malady that made him miss some playing time due to injury.

DOUBLE BONUS

The term "checkmate" comes from the Persian *shah mat,* which means "the king is helpless."

MAKE YOUR OWN REBATES
HOW A SELF-DESCRIBED POOR PERSON GOT CASH BACK

Gary lives at 15615 North 35th Avenue #114 in Phoenix, Arizona. He is very poor. He probably doesn't mind that we're publishing that information, because he gives it out freely. Or, more accurately, he gives it money-ly, if that's a word. (It's not.) Gary writes his address on dollar bills before he spends them. If you end up with one of them, he asks that you mail it back to him.

And it works.

A CBS affiliate in Gary's area tracked him down (not that it was very difficult) to ask him what's going on here. It turns out that Gary is a sixty-something, legally blind retiree. In 2003, he had to take some unpaid leave from his job due to some health issues. That's when he got the idea of asking people to return his money to him. He used a red pen to get the message across. Each dollar bill that passes through his wallet—and he only does this with one-dollar bills—is adorned with a message reading "Please return this bill to me" written at the top, with his address written in the center area around where the word "One" is printed on the bill, and with "I am very poor" at the bottom.

Some do, in fact, come back. He averages about $2 per day in return-to-Gary money and occasionally gets a few extra dollars from particularly generous benefactors. In total, he's seen a few thousand dollars over the years. He's logged all the bills he's received back (whether he declares them as income for tax or benefits purposes, who knows) and where they've come from. In some cases, the money has traveled as far afield as Australia before returning to Arizona.

We don't know Gary's last name—the CBS affiliate declined to publish it—and we don't know how legal the gambit is, either. Title 18 Section 333 of the United States Code states that anyone who (among other things) "mutilates" or "defaces" a dollar bill may be imprisoned for as long as six months, but only if that person did so "with intent to render [the bill] unfit to be reissued." Gary's clear intent is to get spendable money back via the mail (and yes, you can legally send cash through the U.S. Postal Service) and not to render these dollar bills unfit for use. In any case, as of the winter of 2013, Gary hasn't been arrested for his create-your-own-rebate program.

BONUS FACT:

Dollar bills get passed around a lot—so much, in fact, that according to a 2009 report in *National Geographic*, nine out of ten George Washingtons are tainted with cocaine. Microscopic amounts of coke residue get into the bills' fibers during drug deals and after being used by drug snorters as straws, and they remain there as the bills work their way back into circulation.

PENNIES FROM EVERYWHERE
THE COLLEGE STUDENT WHO MICRO-FUNDED HIS OWN SCHOLARSHIP

College tuition is expensive, at least in the United States. The University of California, Los Angeles (UCLA), for example, charges an estimated $33,000 per year (as of 2014) to in-state students who live on campus. That price shoots up to over $56,000 if you hail from outside of California due to "nonresident supplemental tuition." The University of Illinois at Urbana-Champaign (U of I) has a similar price tag, with a base tuition of $35,000 for out-of-staters (and just under $20,000 for in-state students) plus an estimated $10,000 for room, board, and other expenses. That comes to about $30,000 for in-state students, or $45,000 for nonresidents, per year.

So you can see why someone from Illinois would prefer to go to U of I than, say, UCLA. Out of the gate, they're saving roughly half the cost. Still, $27,000 a year for four years is a lot of money. Even with grants and scholarships and student loans available, that's a significant expense for almost anyone. In 1987, a U of I freshman named Mike Hayes figured out a neat way to cut his costs. He asked a columnist at the *Chicago Tribune* to help him find donors to back his education—one penny at a time.

That year, Hayes wrote to columnist Bob Greene with his novel idea. If Hayes could get 2.8 million people to each send him one penny, his tuition, room, board, and the like would be paid for in full. (For a current U of I student, that would be one year's fees. For Hayes, that was for *all four years*.)

It was an outlandish request, sure, but perhaps it played on Greene's ego. (Greene, in 2002, would resign from the *Tribune* in disgrace for having had a sexual encounter fourteen years earlier with a seventeen-year-old student. A CNN personality commented that Greene was "famous for using his position as a columnist . . . to try to get women into bed.") On September 6, 1987, Greene wrote a column-slash-call-to-action, hoping to get those 2.8 million pennies for the young Mr. Hayes. They both realized that the challenge was, probably, foolish:

> Mike Hayes knows—and I know—the real dilemma here.
>
> Right now, every person who is reading this column is thinking, "That's a pretty funny idea. I think I'll send the kid a penny."
>
> But the vast majority of you won't. You'll chuckle, and maybe shake your head, and if someone else is in the room you might mention this to him or her. But then you'll just turn the page and forget about it.
>
> It's not that the penny means anything to you. It's just that getting out of your chair, finding an envelope, addressing it, putting a stamp on it, and remembering to drop it in a mailbox is a lot of trouble.
>
> Well . . . not a lot of trouble. But more trouble than you're willing to deal with.

Twice in the article, Greene posted Hayes's P.O. Box address. When Hayes graduated in 1991, Greene did a follow-up piece. The result: Hayes did not get the 2.8 million pennies. He got far fewer than that—but, to make up for it, he received a bunch of nickels and quarters and even some paper currency and checks. People from all fifty states and a few places overseas sent small donations to Hayes. Most of the money—$23,000 of it—came within the first few weeks. During that short time, the postmaster of Hayes's hometown estimates that Hayes received roughly 70,000 pieces of mail, meaning the average donation was in the thirty-five-cent range, plus another twenty-two cents for postage.

In the end, he collected $29,000—more than enough to cover his education. As for the leftover $1,000, Hayes decided to pay it forward:

> Mike plans to give the extra $1,000 to a deserving college student from one of the families that sent him pennies. "I'm not going to be real scientific about it," he said. "I'm just going to stick my hand into those 90,000 letters we saved, start calling people whose names are on the envelopes I grab, and ask if there's a person in their family who needs $1,000 for college. I'm going to trust them—I'm going to count on them to tell me if they don't really need the college money. If they don't need it, I'll move on to the next envelope."

That's 100,000 pennies, in case you're counting.

BONUS FACT

At the bottom of the Grand Canyon lives a tribe of Native Americans known as the Havasupai. In order for the United States Postal Service to deliver mail to the Havasupai, mail carriers have to travel by mule. Each mule carries approximately 130 pounds of mail and packages down the eight-mile trail daily, totaling about 41,000 pounds each week, according to the USPS. (The Postal Service discontinued the route in mid-2013.) The pennies Hayes was hoping for, 2.8 million, would weigh about seventy-seven tons. It'd take about twenty-six days for the USPS to deliver them to a college student living in the Grand Canyon.

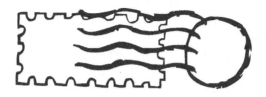

MAY-L
THE CHEAPEST (NOW ILLEGAL) WAY TO SEND YOUR DAUGHTER TO GRANDMA'S HOUSE

On February 19, 1914, a train departed from Grangeville, Idaho. One of its stops was Lewiston, another town in Idaho, located about seventy-five miles to the northwest. There was nothing particularly special about the train that day—no derailments or explosions or heists, and nothing as significant as even a five-minute delay. The train carried passengers and mail, just like it did whenever it ran, and everything and everyone arrived without complaint. Little Charlotte May Pierstorff, a five-year-old girl who was traveling from her parents' house to see her grandma and grandpa, got off the train and was escorted to grandma's without a problem.

Until a government official learned of May's trip.

The problem wasn't that May was a kindergarten-aged girl riding a train without a parent or guardian—that seemed to be no big deal at all, in fact. The problem was that she wasn't a passenger—not technically, at least. A passenger ticket for the ride would have cost her parents roughly a day's wages, which wasn't a viable option for them. Tossing a five-year-old onto a train as a stowaway wasn't an option, either . . . unless one is criminally insane, and there was no reason to believe that Mr. and Mrs. Pierstorff were anything other than good parents. They were resourceful, though, and found another loophole: stick fifty-three cents' worth of stamps on her coat and mail her.

At the time, the U.S. Postal Service would accept any package weighing fifty pounds or less, and little Miss Pierstorff weighed only forty-eight and a half. There were no regulations against sending people through the post—it's probably one of those things that you just assume customers won't do, so why bother having a rule? In this case, the downside of mailing a daughter was pretty low. Sure, she had to ride in the mail compartment, but that was probably a lot of fun for the five-year-old. Arguably, it was safer, since she was aboard the train without a chaperone.

There was another benefit, too. Not only did she get to grandma's house cheaper—it only cost about $12 in today's dollars—but being a piece of mail, the Postal Service wasn't done with the child when the train arrived. While Grandma and Grandpa would have had to pick up May at the train station (or otherwise provide for her continued travel) had she been a normal passenger, that wasn't the case here. The mail clerk on duty in Lewiston, a man named Leonard Mochel, had to deliver her from the train station to her grandmother's house, which he successfully did.

Soon after hearing of Pierstorff's story, the Postmaster General ended the ability of customers to send people through the mail.

BONUS FACT

In 1958, a New York diamond merchant named Harry Winston donated the Hope Diamond to the Smithsonian Institute. At forty-five-and-a-half carats, the gem is worth an estimated $200 million (give or take $50 million), but Winston didn't hire an armored car to deliver it to the Smithsonian. He sent it via the U.S. Postal Service, placing it in a box, wrapping the box in brown paper, and insuring it for $145.29.

EVERY MONTH THEY'RE HUSTLIN'

WHY CONGRESS GETS FREE (AHEM) MEN'S MAGAZINES

Junk mail today usually consists of catalogues offering all sorts of products for sale, but typically, those products are not sexual. In the early to mid-1960s, though, that wasn't the case. It was not uncommon for people to open their mailboxes to find something they wouldn't want their twelve-year-old son to see (even if he really wanted to see it). In the latter part of that decade, the federal government passed a law (39 U.S.C. § 3008 if you'd like to look it up) aiming to help. The new rule: if you received "any pandering advertisement which offers for sale matter which the addressee in his sole discretion believes to be erotically arousing or sexually provocative," you could ask your post office to issue a "prohibitory order"—that is, the Postal Service could make the sender stop sending that stuff to you.

By the early 1980s, the law had been through the legal system and come out perfectly fine, despite a challenge claiming that it violated the senders' First Amendment rights to freedom of speech. So when Larry Flint, the publisher of *Hustler* magazine, started sending his nudie mags to all 535 members of Congress—free and unsolicited—in late 1983, many congressmen asked the post office for prohibitory orders. By October of the following year, 264 of those congressional offices had demanded, via the post office, that their free subscriptions be halted.

Flint stopped, under the advice of counsel, and then sued.

His argument was a First Amendment one, but ultimately it didn't rest on freedom of speech. The First Amendment also guarantees, among other things, the right to petition the government for redress of grievances. Flint argued that he was trying to lead members of Congress to a revelation, opening their eyes to the world around them. As he told *The Hill* magazine in 2011, "Moses freed the Jews, Lincoln freed the slaves, and I just wanted to free all the neurotics."

The court agreed.

So every month, each member of Congress receives a plain manila envelope in the mail containing a few dozen pages of satire, political commentary, and naked women. Most offices file the magazines immediately into the recycling bin. But as one congressional staffer anonymously told *National Journal*, some magazines have been put to a different, arguably better use:

> For a while, the interns, after their initial shock and befuddlement, were directed to save the *Hustlers*. We eventually gave a coworker the whole year's supply for Secret Santa and then she would mail them to her boyfriend in Iraq. Certainly one of the least-heralded ways the office supported our troops.

But yeah, most just throw them out.

BONUS FACT

Larry Flint is no stranger to the courtroom, often litigating First Amendment issues. But his most famous legal battle, *Keeton v. Hustler*, was about the inner workings of the legal system (personal jurisdiction, if your vocabulary includes legal terms of art). He lost and wasn't very happy about it. After losing the case, he temporarily found himself in contempt of court, for, while still in the Supreme Court building and within earshot of the Justices, dropping an f-bomb, calling the eight male Justices a choice word, and referring to Justice Sandra Day O'Connor as a token (highly offensive word that starts with the letter "c"). Charges were dropped shortly thereafter.

NEITHER RAIN NOR SLEET NOR 140,000 POTHOLES
THE TOUGH ROAD TO BECOMING A POSTAL TRUCK

In the United States, people drive on the right side of the road. To make driving and turning easier, the driver usually sits on the left side of the car, placing him or her closer to the center of traffic. There is, however, one notable exception to that latter rule. Mail carriers, in most cases, sit in the right side of their mail trucks—they have to be on the curb side of the vehicle in order to reach mailboxes without having to exit. This feature alone makes mail trucks unique among American motor vehicles. But the differences don't stop there. The white box-shaped trucks you see slowly tootling around the neighborhood have gone through a testing process unlike any other in the area.

The door-to-door mail truck most commonly in use today is called the Grumman LLV, short for Long-Life Vehicle. It was created in the 1980s and is the first vehicle specifically created for the U.S. Postal Service—prior to the LLV, the post office purchased all sorts of available vehicles (often military or government surplus) and repurposed them to serve mail carriers as well as possible. However, the driving needs of a postal truck are much different than almost all other cars out there, so the Postal Service and Grumman worked on a prototype in 1985 to meet those needs.

The tests were rigorous and tedious—as well as bumpy. According to the Smithsonian Institute, the prototypes were subjected to tests that would make most people incredibly carsick. Prototypes had to drive over 2,800 miles while stopping every 250 feet (simulating a whole lot of mailbox deliveries)—that's roughly the equivalent of driving from New York to Los Angeles while stopping more than 60,000 times. The trucks also had to drive more than 10,000 miles over gravel roads at speeds of thirty to forty-five mph and another 1,000 miles over three- to four-inch-high cobblestones, albeit at only ten to fifteen miles per hour. Then there were the potholes: Each of the prototypes' four wheels had to hit at least 35,000 test potholes, often while travelling ten to fifteen miles per hour.

The LLVs are made of corrosion-resistant aluminum and therefore rarely rust. Most cars are made from steel, which is cheaper, but then most cars aren't intended to last as long as mail trucks. Grumman began producing the LLVs in 1987, meeting the U.S. Postal Service's order of 100,000 to 140,000 vehicles (reports vary) within a few years. As it turned out, the Long Life Vehicles really have had long lives. Even though these trucks are still commonly seen in cities and suburbs throughout the United States, Grumman stopped production of them in 1994, meaning that even the newest LLV is two decades old.

The LLVs will be retired soon, though. Not because they no longer work or are too expensive to maintain, but because of environmental concerns. Like most cars of the 1980s and 1990s, they aren't very fuel efficient and will likely be replaced by hybrids or full-electric models over time.

BONUS FACT

In the United States, mail trucks are not required to have (and typically do not have) license plates.

CANNONBALL RUN
THE FASTEST WAY TO DRIVE FROM NEW YORK TO L.A.

If you ask Google Maps how long it will take you to go from New York City to the Los Angeles suburb of Redondo Beach, California, you'll find out that the 2,800-mile trip will take you roughly forty-four hours by car. That's nonstop—no allowances for sleep, meals, bathroom breaks, or even refueling, and certainly no sightseeing. For the vast majority of us, that forty-four-hour estimate for any such cross-country trip is entirely meaningless. We'd take it slow, spreading the trip over at least four days, probably closer to six. We'd stop often along the way, making the trip part of the adventure itself.

For Ed Bolian, the forty-four-hour estimate is similarly meaningless, but for the exact opposite reason. He wanted to get from Manhattan to Redondo Beach is much less time. Two-thirds of the time, in fact.

In 1933, a man named Edwin Baker—"Cannonball" Baker as he'd later become known—made the New York to Los Angeles trip in roughly fifty-three and a half hours, easily a record at the time. (The interstate highway system hadn't been built yet, so Baker's fifty-mile-per-hour average speed was accomplished on county roads and unpaved thoroughfares.) Forty years later, that record still stood. It might have become a small piece of American folklore, mostly forgotten. However, when the 1973 oil crisis hit the American economy, Baker's trip returned to the public eye. The oil shortage led to the creation of a national minimum-speed law of fifty-five miles per hour in hopes of curtailing oil use. In protest, a group of car aficionados organized "Cannonball Run," a cross-country race, as reported by ABC News.

Cannonball Run (which inspired the 1981 movie of the same name) didn't require race organizers or the like—participants just needed to drive from Manhattan to the Portofino Hotel in the Los Angeles area and keep verifiable track of the time. Over the past forty or so years, Baker's record has been replaced many times over. In 1983, two men made the trip in thirty-two hours and seven minutes in a Ferrari 308. That mark stood until 2006, when a guy named Alex Roy led a team that did the trip in thirty-one hours and seven minutes.

Bolian smashed that time.

His attempt in 2013 began a year and a half earlier with the purchase of a Mercedes CL55 AMG. As Jalopnik reported, the car was a good starting point but needed work to make a clearly illegal road trip in record time. First, Bolian added two twenty-two-gallon gas tanks, nearly tripling the car's standard capacity, and a pair of GPS units to make sure he knew where he was at all times. (If one failed, he had a backup.) Most of the work was done to avoid the authorities. The car had multiple iPhone and iPad chargers, allowing for the use of speed trap–dodging apps; a pair of laser jammers (the radar jammer he ordered wasn't finished in time), a kill switch for the rear lights, and three radar detectors. He also added a CB radio so he could ask trucks to slow down in order to pass them—masquerading, via radio, as a trucker himself.

He didn't make the trip alone, of course. He had a codriver, whom he recruited only a few weeks before the run, and a spotter in the back seat—his job was to watch for cops and calculate fuel needs—who joined the team just days before the record-breaking attempt. On October 19, 2013, the trio left Manhattan . . .

. . . and promptly got stuck in traffic. It took fifteen minutes to get off the island.

Nevertheless, it was basically smooth sailing from there on out. Over the next twenty-eight hours and change, the trio sped their way to the greater Los Angeles area, averaging—averaging!—ninety-eight miles per hour the entire time. Yes, that includes gas and bathroom breaks.

BONUS FACT

In 2011, a pair of New Yorkers made another notable trans-America trip—a slow one, taking six days and costing them thousands of dollars. As the *Daily Mail* reported, two guys hailed a taxi outside of New York City's LaGuardia Airport and negotiated a deal with the cab driver to drive them all the way to L.A. at the discounted rate of $5,000. (By mileage, the fare should have been at least twice that.) Why? One of the two passengers was the son of a former cabbie and wanted to show his dad that you could, in fact, hail a taxi to take you to California—he figured actually making the trip was the best proof.

LIFE IN THE FAST LANE
WHY RICH PEOPLE SHOULDN'T SPEED IN FINLAND

Speeding may earn you a ticket. In most cases, it will cost you maybe $150 in America or 100 Euros in Europe. For many people, that could be the difference between making this month's rent and being in arrears. For others, it's barely noticeable.

So Finland tried to fix it. Which is why, in 2001, Finland fined Anssi Vanjoki, a high-paid Nokia executive, more than $100,000 for driving seventy-five kilometers per hour (forty-seven miles per hour) in a fifty-kph (thirty-one-mph) zone.

In 1921, Finland adopted a "day-fine" law, which aimed to apply the ecumenical effect of incarceration to petty violations such as littering and minor traffic violations. Finland noted that jail time hit the rich and poor roughly equally; for each day in prison, the convict lost a day of freedom, whether rich or poor. Fines, the government concluded, should follow a similar framework. Since that year, those infractions can cost a violator a whole day's pay—be it fifty Euros or 50,000 Euros. And unlike other countries with day-fine laws, Finland has no maximum fine amounts.

As reported by the BBC, for Vanjoki, this meant a bill of 116,000 Euros (at the time, about $103,000). In October 2001, he was riding his motorcycle fifteen miles per hour over the speed limit and, when caught, was given a fine equal to fourteen days of his annual income, which is how the day-fine system should work. But Vanjoki's case had an odd wrinkle—it was based on his income for the 1999 filing year, which was much higher than typical. Vanjoki appealed the fine, arguing that in 1999 he sold a number of stock options, boosting his income tremendously. By 2001 he was making significantly less money because his equity stake in Nokia was worth much less. The courts agreed with him and cut his fine by 95 percent.

While the day-fine system seems more fair than the typical flat-fine system most of the world uses, it has found its critics. England and Wales tried it in the early 1990s, but it was generally disliked due to the difference between fines. (The BBC noted one example of two men ticketed for fighting each other; the fine levied on the richer of the two was ten times that of the poorer.) In 2002, American economist Steven Landsburgh took to the *Wall Street Journal* to assail the scheme by pointing out an absurd result: "If Mr. Vanjoki speeds while his chauffeur rides in the passenger seat, the price is $100,000. If they switch seats, the price drops to $50."

BONUS FACT

Another Finnish innovation? The dish-draining closet. These are cupboards situated above the kitchen sink with a hole at the bottom. They're designed to allow people to place recently washed dishes right back into the cabinet without drying them first. The dishwater then drips down, slowly, into the sink below. Invented in the mid-1940s, the dish-draining closet was named "one of the most important Finnish innovations of the millennium," according to Wikipedia.

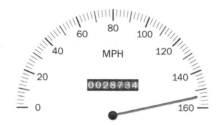

TO COLLECT AND SERVE
THE SMALL TOWN RUNNING A FULL-TIME SCAM

In 1947, the inhabitants of a three-block residential area in Ohio decided to incorporate as a municipality called the village of New Rome. By the year 2000, the village had grown—but only slightly. It encompassed two-hundredths of a square mile, and per the census that year was home to sixty people. Nevertheless, fourteen of the sixty were police officers who patrolled the area and its one main road—and the village leaders apparently wanted even more officers. The reason? The New Rome speed trap, a notorious feature of Ohio travel, and a lucrative one for the tiny village.

West Broad Street, a relatively busy roadway, runs through the area. Decades ago, it was the main road coming out of the state capital of Columbus, five or ten miles away, before I-70 was built in the late 1950s and the 1960s. Nevertheless, it still has a steady flow of traffic—one that New Rome treated like a honey pot. The posted speed limit on West Broad is forty-five miles per hour, but until 2003, the tiny section that ran through New Rome had a lower speed limit of thirty-five miles per hour. The well-staffed New Rome police force watched the area nearly around the clock with ticket books at the ready, waiting for the inevitable speeding violations caused by the sudden drop-off.

The program was quite lucrative. In an average year, New Rome brought in $400,000 in gross revenue through traffic tickets. But the volume of the tickets issued wasn't the only reason why the village made so much money—zealous (overzealous, likely) enforcement was also a key element. Almost all the ticketed drivers lived outside of New Rome, but that didn't stop the small village from taking extreme measures to enforce the tickets. As *Car and Driver* reported, "Once stopped, drivers [were] routinely asked where they work. Fail to pay the fine on time, and a New Rome cop or two may appear at your work place the day after, handcuff you in front of the boss, and haul you off for payment discussions."

A $90 fine for speeding wasn't the only thing drivers were typically faced with. If you were pulled over in New Rome, there was a good chance that you'd find yourself on the wrong end of a laundry list of fines. Have tinted windows? Tack on another $105. No front license plate? $55 more. Make an unsafe lane change—and you can imagine how subjective that is—another $90. In total, you could be ticketed for more than a dozen various violations as officers conveniently found ways to run up the tab.

The good news for travelers along this route? The speed traps are gone. For that matter, so is the entire village of New Rome—but not because of the abusive traffic controls. In 1979, New Rome held an election for village council and never did so after that. The council members—almost all members of the same family—just kept re-appointing one another to vacant seats, arguing that the others in the municipality weren't interested in running. Further, the state of Ohio noted, the village didn't actually provide many (if any) meaningful services to the public. Most were provided at the township, county, or state level. Based on these factors, the state forcibly dissolved the village (over the protests of many of

New Rome's residents) and mandated that it be absorbed into the surrounding township.

BONUS FACT

In 2010, the Supreme Court of Ohio decided that police officers do not need to use radar guns to determine if you've been speeding—they just need experience. According to a report by ABC News, the court ruled that "a police officer's unaided visual estimation of a vehicle's speed is sufficient evidence to support a conviction for speeding . . . if the officer is properly trained." Soon thereafter the state legislature passed a law requiring the use of actual speed detection devices.

HOLY TOLEDO
WHEN OHIO AND MICHIGAN ALMOST WENT TO WAR

Ask any college football fan about rivalries, and the long-standing friendly (okay, not so friendly) "hatred" between Michigan and Ohio State will undeniably make their list. The annual matchup, once ranked by ESPN as the top rivalry in sports, dates back to 1897 with more than 100 gridiron battles since.

But Michigan and Ohio once went to war—real war, with militias, and perhaps even bayonets and horses.

Ohio became a state in 1803. Two years later, the U.S. government formed the Michigan Territory, a pre-statehood area encompassing the modern states of Michigan, Wisconsin, Minnesota, Iowa, and parts of North and South Dakota. However, map-making at the time wasn't all that great. Maps were often best guesses as to the true geography and topography of the area, and when reality struck in late 1834 or early 1835, it turned out to be different from what the maps suggested. A nearly 500-square-mile strip of land between Michigan and Ohio, dubbed the "Toledo Strip" after the major city in the area, was suddenly in dispute. Both sides wanted the land, particularly because it was clear that the location of Toledo was perfect for a port city, and therefore, an economic boon awaited the ultimate owner.

In April 1835, President Andrew Jackson tried to stave off the conflict. Unfortunately, he, too, was conflicted. He asked his attorney general to investigate whether Michigan's or Ohio's claim was legally correct, but quickly realized that Ohio—like now—was a "swing state" in the presidential election. He decided that it'd be best to appease Ohioans and give them the Strip, hoping to entice them to vote for the Democratic candidate in the 1836 election. However, Jackson's attorney general reported back with contrary findings, concluding that Michigan's claim would carry the day. Jackson decided to try and pull an end-around, asking to re-survey the line (with the expectation that the new survey would put the Strip in Ohio). Michigan, flatly, said no.

Unable to settle the issue amicably, the two sides raised militias and occupied the area—the Michigan forces on one side of a key river, and Ohio's on the other. Thankfully, few shots were fired, most of them warning shots aimed at the sky. The only bloodshed in the entire months-long skirmish occurred on July 15, 1835, when Joseph Wood, a Michigan sheriff, went into Toledo to arrest Benjamin Stickney, an Ohioan major, for trespassing on Michigan soil. One of Stickney's sons (named Two—really) stabbed Wood with a penknife; the wound was not fatal.

With hostilities boiling and on the brink of eruption, Jackson tried again to resolve the conflict. In June 1836, he signed an act that would allow the Michigan territory to become a state, under the condition that it ceded any claim to the Toledo Strip to Ohio. (As part of the deal, Michigan would get most of what is now known as the Upper Peninsula.) Michigan again refused, and it seemed an escalation of the war was likely. Ohio had authorized $300,000 to raise its militia; Michigan one-upped Ohio by authorizing $315,000 for similar efforts.

This last action ended the "war"—not because Michigan now had the better militia, but because it had more debt. At the close of 1836 the Michigan territory was teetering on bankruptcy and, not being a state, was not eligible for a 5 percent commission on the sale of federal lands, which would have netted Michigan roughly half a million dollars. The federal government was running a budgetary surplus at the time, and $400,000 was to be distributed to the states—but Michigan wasn't one yet.

On December 14, 1836, Michigan accepted Jackson's terms. In January, it became the twenty-sixth state in the Union. A month earlier, in the presidential election, Martin Van Buren, a Democrat (like Andrew Jackson), won—but not because of Andrew Jackson's efforts in Ohio. Ohio's electoral delegates voted for William Henry Harrison, the Whig candidate.

BONUS FACT

While Martin Van Buren won the presidency, his running mate, Richard Mentor Johnson, failed to win the vice presidential election outright. That year, there were 294 available votes in the Electoral College; to win, a candidate needed 148 or more. Van Buren received 170 and won the presidency without controversy. But the twenty-three electors from Virginia who voted for Van Buren refused to also cast their ballots for Johnson. Johnson received only 147 votes, and fell one shy of the 148 needed. As required by the Constitution, the election then went to the U.S. Senate, which ended up electing Johnson anyway.

THE WAR OF MARBLE HILL
"THE AMERICAN SUDETENLAND"

When many people think of New York City, they focus on the borough of Manhattan, the island that features the Empire State Building, Central Park, Grand Central Terminal, and other things nonresidents know about. There are four other boroughs—Brooklyn, Queens, Staten Island, and the Bronx—but to get from any of those to Manhattan, you have to take a bridge or tunnel, with the rare exception of a neighborhood called Marble Hill. It's not part of Manhattan Island—rather, it is connected to the Bronx. But if you're voting or called for jury duty, you do so as a Manhattan resident.

Its history gives us a brief glimpse into America's early attitude toward Adolf Hitler and the Nazis.

Manhattan is separated from the Bronx by the Harlem River, which connects the Hudson River to the East River. In 1890, a section of the Harlem River that was a few thousand yards from the Hudson was very narrow, and seafaring vessels had difficulty in navigating it. The Army Corps of Engineers decided to reroute the Harlem River, creating a wider passageway south. In doing so, it cut off a piece of Manhattan—Marble Hill—turning it into an island.

When the county of the Bronx was created by the state on January 1, 1914, Marble Hill—still an island—was officially included as part of Manhattan. Unfortunately for mapmakers everywhere, the old path of the Harlem River fell into disuse and was filled in sometime during that same year. Marble Hill was, from that point on, a neighborhood in Manhattan that was paradoxically attached to the Bronx but not to Manhattan itself.

For more than two decades, no one seemed bothered by this. However, in 1939, Bronx borough president James F. Lyons tried to capitalize on this curiosity and turn it into some publicity for himself. He went to the neighborhood—"unarmed and escorted only by his chauffeur," in the words of the *New York Times*—and climbed to the summit of a rocky hill, where he planted the flag of Bronx County. Symbolically, he was claiming the neighborhood for his borough. While residents of Marble Hill jeered him, Lyons was unperturbed, comparing himself to Abraham Lincoln and noting that some disliked Honest Abe for freeing the slaves.

The news media ate it up, just as Lyons had hoped. The *Times* article featured a picture of him, grinning widely, holding the Bronx County flag on a rock atop the hill, his chauffeur-assistant standing stoically next to him. Everyone seemed to appreciate the joke, but the *Times*, for some reason, did not carry Lyons's self-comparison to Abe Lincoln. Instead, they saw a different person in Lyons, one who doesn't seem so funny to modern ears: Adolf Hitler.

The *Times* casually referred to him as "the Bronx Fuehrer" multiple times in its coverage of his "bloodless coup" the next day. Further, the *Times* called Marble Hill the Bronx's "Sudetenland," a reference to the section of Czechoslovakia that the Nazis had annexed a year prior. All of this was done tongue-in-cheek, of course, but apparently in the spring of 1939, it was perfectly okay for a major U.S. publication to jokingly liken an American politician to Adolf Hitler.

As for Marble Hill itself, the attempted annexation failed—it had no lasting impact on the geography of New York City. To this day, the neighborhood remains a part of Manhattan, although residents go to schools in the Bronx and are serviced by Bronx-based emergency responders.

BONUS FACT

On the day of Lyons's attempted annexation of Marble Hill, reporters thought that he had brought in reinforcements—there were four tanks sitting near the border between the neighborhood and the Bronx. It turns out that was a coincidence. An enterprising entrepreneur had bought fourteen surplus tanks from the government and was shipping them to South America to be used as tractors. Ten of the fourteen had already been shipped, but the other four were sitting there, unmanned and uninvolved, as Lyons and his driver invaded Marble Hill.

REVERSE CARTOGRAPHY
THE MAP THAT PREDATED THE TOWN

Travelers starting in the New York City area and making their way across New York State—perhaps to a resort in the Catskills or to Binghamton University—may stop at the Roscoe Diner. It sits on Route 17, one of the main thoroughfares between the city and points westward, and has a reputation extending for miles, in part because you can get some very good French toast there. Otherwise, you are in the middle of nowhere. Roscoe, the town (and it's not really a town, but a "census designated place"), has only 900 or so residents. The nearby municipality of Agloe has even fewer: no one lives there.

But that's because it only kind of exists.

If two companies make a map of the same area but do so independent of each other, the maps should have some identical data. Towns and roads and bodies of water need to be represented accurately or drivers and others using the maps to navigate their surroundings will certainly get lost. Sure, you can be creative when it comes to choice of colors, fonts, or line thickness, but the locations of things have to be right or the map won't be very useful.

As a consequence of this, it's very easy for a third party to start making maps—the mapmaker simply has to copy the data from any other reliable map and reproduce it. To some degree, copyright law should prevent this, but outright copying isn't so easy to prove. As a solution, some mapmakers add fake streets (called "trap streets") or even fake towns (often called "paper towns") into their maps. Any third party copying their work will also copy the fictional creation unique to the original mapmaker's product.

According to novelist and YouTube celeb John Green in a TEDx talk, the General Drafting Company in 1937 did just this with the town of Agloe, creating it out of thin air at the intersection of two dirt roads just a few miles from Roscoe. (Green later used Agloe as one of the locations for his novel, *Paper Towns*, and as the inspiration for its title.) A few decades later, Agloe appeared again, but this time in a map made by a different, unrelated company—Rand McNally. General Drafting thought they had caught Rand McNally red-handed, but Rand McNally had a good and surprising defense:

The county clerk's office had given them the information.

It turns out that, in the early part of the 1950s, someone armed with the General Drafting map went to visit Agloe. Seeing nothing there, he figured that opportunity had knocked. This lost-to-history fellow probably guessed that others would also come to Agloe—it was on the map, after all!—and would expect to find something there. So he opened a small shop and called it the Agloe General Store. Over the next forty years, the fictional town of Agloe grew. As Green notes, at its largest, Agloe had a gas station, the general store, and two houses. Most importantly, Agloe had the attention of the county administrators. They considered Agloe a real place, and therefore, so did Rand McNally's team of cartographers.

Today, sadly, Agloe is gone. The buildings are abandoned if not destroyed, and the mapmakers of the world no longer recognize its existence.

BONUS FACT

Orbiting the Earth right now is a satellite called LAGEOS 1, which contains a plaque designed by the late astronomer Carl Sagan. The plaque is effectively a map, showing what the arrangement of the continents looked like when the satellite was placed into orbit. Why include this? LAGEOS 1 is expected to return to Earth in about 8 million years (due to orbital decay), and when it does, the map will tell whomever or whatever discovers it the epoch from which it came.

A PERFECTLY CROMULENT WORD
THE VERY BRIEF HISTORY OF TWO WORDS THAT AREN'T

"A noble spirit embiggens the smallest man," said Jebediah Spring-field, the namesake and founder of the hometown of Homer and Marge Simpson's family. The word "embiggen," of course, isn't a word at all, despite the assertion of schoolteacher Miss Hoover that it is a "perfectly cromulent word." (It shouldn't surprise anyone that "cromulent" is, also, a made-up nonword.) One can say that Mr. Springfield's esquivalience in formulating a motto for his town via a well-known speech was disappointing. After all, one would think that Jebediah's investment in the region and in his own legacy would have compelled him to invest the time needed to craft a mes-sage involving, you know, actual words. But it wasn't to be. The dord of fake words attributed to him is, therefore, incredibly high.

And yes, "esquivalience" is made up, too. Same with "dord." You can find both in a dictionary, though, if you look hard enough—but for two very different reasons.

First came "dord," courtesy of the G. and C. Merriam Company (a predecessor of Merriam-Webster). "Dord" first appeared in its 1934 edition of the *New International Dictionary* as a noun from the disciplines of physics and chemistry, meaning "density." The error was due to odd typesetting at the time. The entry was supposed to be "D or d"—that is, a capital or lowercase letter D—the dictionary noting that either could be used, in physics or chemistry, as an abbreviation for "density." But the entry was set as "D o r d," and a later editor removed what appeared to be three unnecessary spaces.

"Dord" remained in subsequent editions through 1939, when a proofreader realized that the word lacked an etymology and called its veracity into question. Other dictionaries used the word until 1947, likely having copied from old dictionaries (including, perhaps, those of competitors). This may have inspired the creation of "esquivalence."

"Esquivalence" was first spotted in the 2001 edition of the *New Oxford American Dictionary* (NOAD), a noun meaning "the willful avoidance of one's official responsibilities; the shirking of duty." It was crafted by an editor named Christine Lindberg, according to the *New Yorker*, and was included for the sole purpose of catching those who copied the NOAD team's work. This was more than a matter of pride—if the word appeared in another publication, NOAD immediately had evidence that the second dictionary had violated NOAD's copyright.

Which is exactly what happened. The "word" appeared on Dictionary.com, which attributed it to *Webster's New Millennium Dictionary*, but it was removed from both after the ruse was revealed. The Oxford team didn't pursue any legal action against either company.

BONUS FACT

The Simpsons debuted in 1989; with that debut came the repeated utterance of Homer's catchphrase, "D'oh!," another fabricated word. However, unlike "embiggen" and "cromulent," this one has slowly crept into common parlance. The *Oxford English Dictionary*'s editors recognized this in 2001, adding "d'oh" to their dictionary. It means, "Expressing frustration at the realization that things have turned out badly or not as planned, or that one has just said or done something foolish."

THE CHART TOPPER
THE BESTSELLING BOOK THAT YOU COULDN'T BUY

Bestseller lists are self-explanatory: Books make the list when lots of people buy them. Sell enough, you make the list. Pretty straightforward stuff. There are wrinkles, of course. For example, a book will often crack the bestseller list even before it hits shelves, as presales vault the tome into notoriety. That's what happened in 1956, when the book *I, Libertine* by Frederick R. Ewing made the *New York Times* bestseller list before publication. It was a coup for Mr. Ewing, who not only had never written a book before but also didn't exist.

For that matter, neither did the book.

The credit—or perhaps, blame—goes to a late-night radio host named Jean Shepherd. Shepherd is probably best known for his story collection *In God We Trust, All Others Pay Cash*, which was later adapted into the movie *A Christmas Story* (which Shepherd himself narrated). In this case, he wanted to pull a prank, one designed to show how silly bestseller lists were.

He asked his listeners to go into bookstores across the country and order the aforementioned book by Mr. Ewing, and he provided his listeners with a loosely established plot outline in case bookstore clerks were looking for more information. The prank was intended to simply confuse a bookseller or two. Shepherd believed the stores would inform the customers that no such title existed; that's what happened to him when he tried to buy a book of old radio scripts that, apparently, had never been printed.

But that's not what happened. The book—the nonexistent book—took on a life of its own. Even though it didn't exist, book clubs and book reviewers were talking about it, according to listeners who called in to Shepherd's radio show. In a later interview about the hoax, Shepherd noted that a church in Boston had added the book to the proscribed list, banning parishioners from reading it. The attention around the book was so great that many retailers asked their book buyers about the title and in doing so, caught the eye of industry experts. This surge in popularity earned the title the notice of the bestseller lists, and, perhaps more importantly, of Ian Ballantine, publisher of Ballantine Books. Ballantine tracked down the mysterious origins of the title and contacted Shepherd.

Ballantine, Shepherd, and novelist Thomas Sturgeon met for lunch and discussed making Shepherd's joke into a real book. A few months later, *I, Libertine*—a 151-page novel in both paperback and hardcover—hit bookstores across the country. The *Wall Street Journal* ran a front-page article about the hoax, so there was little risk of any readers being bamboozled, and in any event, the proceeds of the book went to charity.

BONUS FACT

The house where *A Christmas Story* was filmed is now a museum, open to the public year-round. (It's in Cleveland, if you're inclined to visit.) The movie notably features a lamp that looks like a woman's leg clad in a fishnet stocking. According to the museum's website, the lamp was custom-made for the movie, and only three were produced. All three were destroyed during movie production.

THE VERY BAD EGG
THE MISSING CHILD FROM
CHARLIE AND THE CHOCOLATE FACTORY

In 1964, Roald Dahl published his third book, *Charlie and the Chocolate Factory*. Seven years later, in 1971, it was made into a hit movie, *Willy Wonka & the Chocolate Factory*, starring Gene Wilder. The story is that of a poor child, Charlie Bucket, who lucks into a golden ticket, one that entitles him (and his Grandpa Joe) entry into Willy Wonka's famous chocolate factory. Four other children also find golden tickets and join Charlie on the tour.

One by one, each child (other than Charlie) suffers an odd fate. The obese Augustus Gloop, unable to control his love of chocolate, falls into a river of chocolate and is sucked into a pipe—to be made into fudge. Another, compulsive gum chewer Violet Beauregarde, turns into an ever-expanding human blueberry, filling with blueberry juice. A third, the bratty Veruca Salt, is judged a "bad nut" (in the movie, the nuts are changed to eggs) and sent off to the furnace. The fourth, television addict (and aptly named) Mike Teavee, shrinks himself in a television transportation device. Only Charlie avoids a horrific accident. And all the children but Charlie are, on their way out of the factory, serenaded. Wonka's servants, the green-haired, orange-faced Oompa-Loompas, gleefully marked the occasion of each child's fall from grace with a song and dance.

Miranda Piker—the straight-laced daughter of a school headmaster—was child number six. Her story did not make the final version of the book. In Dahl's original draft, Wonka develops a candy that makes the child break out in spots—a fake illness designed to get the child out of a day of school. Piker objects and she and her schoolmaster father storm the room in which the candy is being made. Something explodes, and Piker and her father, by Wonka's scheme, are turned into a necessary part of the recipe: "We've got to use one or two schoolmasters occasionally or it wouldn't work," he says.

Piker's story was cut, since the book publishers believed it to be too gruesome for young audiences. But a few years ago, the *Times* (UK) obtained and printed the excerpt, complete with the Oompa-Loompas' song, which can be found on the *Times* website as of May 2014.

BONUS FACT

The actor who played Charlie in *Willy Wonka & the Chocolate Factory* is named Peter Ostrum. It was his only movie. He was offered the opportunity to reprise the role in two sequels but turned it down, saying that acting was more difficult than it was glamorous. (As it turned out, there'd be no second or third movies anyway; Dahl hated the first movie so much, he refused to allow the sequel, *Charlie and the Great Glass Elevator*, to be adapted for the screen, and he died before writing the third part in the series.) Later in life, Ostrum became a large-animal veterinarian, a profession he still practices today.

WORTHY OF GRYFFINDOR
HOW TO BECOME FRIENDS WITH HARRY POTTER

By the time *Harry Potter and the Goblet of Fire*, the fourth book in the Harry Potter saga, was published in 2000, the series had already become a smashing success. The first book, *Harry Potter and the Philosopher's Stone* ("Sorcerer's Stone" in the United States) debuted in the UK in the summer of 1997 and was being turned into a movie; the *Goblet of Fire* book set a new record for Amazon .com pre-orders. Its popularity rampant, Potter's trials and tribulations won fans of all kinds. Among them was Natalie McDonald of Toronto, a nine-year-old girl who could not wait to hear how the story would end—but sadly, not because she was impatient. McDonald had a terminal case of leukemia and was all but certain to die before *Goblet* hit the bookstores.

A family friend, Annie Kidder, went to the publisher of the Potter series, asking them to pass a letter (and fax) on to J.K. Rowling, author of the books. Kidder's request was a simple one: give this dying child a preview of the outcome of *Goblet*—nearly a year before the rest of the world would be able to read it—as the *Potter* stories "had been [Natalie's] respite from the hell of leukemia" and Natalie was not going to survive long enough to otherwise enjoy the story.

Rowling was on vacation when the request arrived and replied via e-mail to Natalie's mother on August 4, 1999. The e-mail detailed the fate of the main characters in *Goblet of Fire* and did so eleven months prior to the book's publication date. Unfortunately, Natalie passed away the day prior to receiving the news.

Nevertheless, Natalie's mother Valerie and Rowling began a friendship from that day forward. Rowling, for her part, honored Natalie's memory in print—on page 159 (or 180, depending on the version) of *Goblet of Fire*, a young witch by the name of Natalie McDonald, new to Hogwarts, dons the Sorting Hat and becomes a member of House Gryffindor.

BONUS FACT

Perhaps Rowling was paying the favor forward. She completed the manuscript for *Philosopher's Stone* in 1995 but two years and twelve rejection letters later had failed to find a publisher. In 1997, a small UK publishing house decided to take a chance on the then-unknown author when Alice Newton read the first chapter and demanded that the company publish the manuscript so that she would be able to read the rest of the story. Who was Alice Newton? The eight-year-old daughter of the company's chairman.

BLUE MAN GROUP
WHY CIVIL WAR SOLDIERS GLOWED IN THE DARK

Photorhabdus luminescens sounds like a spell from the Harry Potter universe, maybe one that lights up a camera or ignites whatever mythical creature a "habdus" might be. In fact, the wizards and witches of Hogwarts aside, *Photorhabdus luminescens* was once the cause of what many likely considered magic. Just ask Confederate soldiers during the U.S. Civil War—especially the ones who inexplicably began to glow in the dark.

In April 1862, Union and Confederate forces met at Shiloh, Tennessee. The Battle of Shiloh was a clear Northern victory despite a heavy casualty count on both sides—each had roughly 1,700 soldiers dead and another 8,000 wounded. The Confederate medical crews were ill-prepared for those types of casualties, and many wounded Southerners were, therefore, left untreated for a few days. When night came, the wounds of some of the injured soldiers, still left unattended, began emanating a faint blue light. They created a soft glow in the otherwise-dark battlefield. When the wounded soldiers finally received treatment, many claimed that those who had the glowing injuries healed more thoroughly than those without the apparently supernatural halo.

It wasn't a gift from the heavens, of course. It came from *Photorhabdus luminescens*, a type of bacteria. *P. luminescens*, as the cool kids call it, is a bioluminescent microbe that has a symbiotic relationship with roundworms, a parasitic nematode that infects insects. The roundworm invades an insect and, effectively, throws up a gut full of *P. luminescens*. The bacteria releases a toxin that kills the insect within forty-eight hours and an enzyme that breaks down the insect's body. The nematode then eats the liquefied insect, returning much of the bacteria to its home inside the roundworm's body.

The roundworms—and therefore the bacteria—were most likely present in the mud and dirt of the Shiloh battlefield. It's further likely that the microbes made their way into the wounds of many of the injured Confederate soldiers and, because of other conditions, were able to thrive there. Even that required a bit of luck, which explains why only some of the soldiers began to glow.

While *P. luminescens* typically can't survive in a human host because our body temperature is too warm for them, according to MentalFloss.com, prolonged exposure to the rainy and wet conditions of the battlefield caused many soldiers to suffer from hypothermia. This dropped the body temperature of those fighters, allowing *P. luminescens* to invade their wounds—and, being a bioluminescent creature with a blueish hue, to create the glow.

The good news for those soldiers is that *P. luminescens* isn't all that infectious, and our bodies' immune systems can typically handle the microbe. But before that happens, the *P. luminescens* do their human hosts a favor typically reserved for the roundworms. The toxins they produce that kill insects also happen to kill other bacteria in the area, keeping the *P. luminescens* and its host safe from infection. That's almost certainly what happened in this case, which is why the glowing soldiers recovered more quickly than their standard-hued comrades-at-arms.

BONUS FACT

The gene of *P. luminescens* associated with the insect-killing toxin was discovered by a team of British researchers in 2002. They named the gene "mcf"—short for "make caterpillars floppy," because that's what the toxin does.

MISTER BEER BELLY
HOW TO ACCIDENTALLY BREW
BEER WHEREVER YOU ARE

The human body contains roughly 10 trillion cells—and roughly 100 trillion bacteria. These bacteria—life forms in their own right—constitute as much as 2 percent of our body mass. Most of the bacteria operate, effectively, independent of us, having little to no effect on our health or well-being. Some are actually symbiotic, aiding in the digestion of food and perhaps even making us smarter (although that study is controversial). Others are harmful—one type may make depression symptoms worse—while others cause illnesses such as strep throat.

And others turn our stomachs into breweries.

Well, once at least.

Sometime in the late summer or early fall of 2013, a sixty-one-year-old Texas man walked into an emergency room drunk out of his mind. Nurses administered a Breathalyzer exam and determined that the patient's blood-alcohol level was 0.37 (which can lead to serious impairment). Normally he'd be given some time to sober up. But there was one weird variable in this case: the man hadn't been drinking. To make sure that he wasn't sneaking a shot or two, doctors searched him for booze and, finding none, stuck him in a hospital room, alone, for twenty-four hours. He was given food like any other patient as medical professionals kept monitoring his blood-alcohol level. While people who had stopped drinking and eaten some food would sober up, the man actually got drunker. His blood-alcohol level went up 12 percent.

The cause was a microbe known as *Saccharomyces cerevisiae*, more commonly known as "baker's yeast" or "brewer's yeast." As the Environmental Protection Agency notes, not only is the microorganism typically harmless, but it's also particularly useful. It has been used for centuries as a leavening agent for bread and a fermenting agent for alcohol. *Saccharomyces cerevisiae* infections are unheard of, as the microbe almost always passes through the human body without issue.

In this case, though, something was amiss. As NPR reported, a significant amount of *Saccharomyces cerevisiae* had taken residence in the patient's gut. The reasons why were unclear, but the result— termed "auto-brewery syndrome"—was striking. Whenever the man ate anything starchy—"a bagel, pasta, or even soda" are the examples NPR gave—the man was also feeding the *Saccharomyces cerevisiae*. The microbe churned through the carbohydrates and released ethanol as a byproduct. The man was brewing beer in his own stomach and getting drunk from it.

The two doctors who discovered this curiosity published a paper on the topic in the *International Journal of Clinical Medicine*, but as others have pointed out, the doctors didn't perform a controlled study nor did they have more than one person—and therefore more than one data point—to work from. Why the *Saccharomyces cerevisiae* took root in the man's stomach remains unknown, but it's treatable—an antifungal medicine called fluconazole will kill off the intrusive microbes. (Sorry—despite this, fluconazole probably won't help you sober up after a night out.)

BONUS FACT

Craft brewing is apparently of particular importance to the people of the state of Oregon. How do we know this? Because in May 2013, the Oregon legislature passed a law making *Saccharomyces cerevisiae* the state's official microbe, in light of the microbe's work in creating beer. (Every state needs an official microbe, right?)

LIQUOR, SICKER
THE NEFARIOUS PLOT TO ENFORCE PROHIBITION

The Eighteenth Amendment to the United States Constitution went into effect in 1919, and early the next year Prohibition began when the Volstead Act became law. The sale, manufacture, or transportation of alcohol became unlawful and would remain illegal until 1933, when the Twenty-First Amendment repealed the Eighteenth. During the interim, however, alcohol-related illnesses and deaths were common. These maladies were the byproduct of speakeasies and moonshine, both of which were cloaked from the law, and therefore the injured were out of the reach of legal remedy.

There was another cause of alcohol-related death during Prohibition: poisoning by the U.S. government.

With alcohol illegal, Prohibition created a huge opportunity for organized crime to enter the market. The lucrative business of bootlegging (the transport of illegal alcohol) created an economic foundation for Al Capone and his gang in Chicago as well as other notorious criminals. Because the sale of all alcohol was illegal, it made good business sense for criminals to focus on hard liquor, which could be made from (legal) industrial ethyl alcohol and therefore had a large profit margin. The problem: industrial alcohol was basically grain alcohol mixed with a solvent or two, making it undrinkable.

The bootleggers hired chemists to fix that, and the chemists succeeded. Before long, illegal but barely palatable booze, derived from industrial alcohol, was flowing throughout speakeasies and the like all across the United States.

The Department of the Treasury, which was charged with enforcement of the Volstead Act, had a solution: They added even more poison to the mix. The bootleggers were unable to make the alcohol entirely safe for drinking, but of course, many bootleggers were murderous criminals—and they sold the liquor anyway. The Treasury's plan failed to stem the tide of alcohol flowing in the streets but did sadly manage to claim the lives of as many as 10,000 people.

BONUS FACT

Prohibition turned many citizens into everyday criminals, many by way of homemade wine. Grocers could sell grape concentrate, an item that in and of itself lacked any alcohol. However, if treated in a certain way, grape concentrate would ferment, turning it into wine. In order to "avoid" this outcome, many grape concentrate packages were labeled with a warning—outlining exactly what not to do in order to ensure that your grape concentrate did not ferment.

VODKA AND COLA
HOW TO SMUGGLE COKE INTO SOVIET RUSSIA

In 1992, with an incredible amount of fanfare, Pepsi announced Crystal Pepsi, a clear cola beverage aimed at revolutionizing the soft-drink world. The drink did well initially and even spurred Coca-Cola to come out with its own clear cola product, called Tab Clear. Neither beverage would survive commercially for very long. Crystal Pepsi was off shelves in the United States by the end of 1993; according to Fast Company, one of the executives behind the concept later admitted that the product just didn't taste good. Tab Clear, somehow, persevered into the middle of 1994. Its marketing was suspect—for some reason, it was only sold in a can, a curious choice for a beverage whose main selling point was the fact that it was translucent.

Given these failures, one would assume that these massive soft-drink companies had never before attempted to make a cola that wasn't caramel-colored. But well before Crystal Pepsi and Tab Clear came another different-colored cola, informally called White Coke.

In the 1940s, the Marshal of the Soviet Union (the de facto highest rank in the Soviet military), a man named Georgy Zhukov, took a liking to Coca-Cola. However, Coke was symbolic of

America, of capitalism, etc., and Zhukov—given his position of prominence—couldn't be seen drinking the stuff. Through his American counterpart General Mark W. Clark (who in turn took the question to President Truman), Zhukov asked that the Coca-Cola Company develop a cola that visually resembled vodka. This way, the *New York Times* reported, he could be seen drinking it whenever he liked, without risking the ire of Joseph Stalin. (Apparently, it was okay for Soviet military leaders to have a vodka.) Coke complied.

For years, Coke provided the cola to Zhukov and somehow managed to avoid most of the red tape that defined importations into the USSR during that period. The cola was never introduced to consumers in the States.

BONUS FACT

In 1990, the Mars candy company introduced PB Max, a cookie topped with peanut butter, and the whole thing covered in milk chocolate. Like Crystal Pepsi and Tab Clear, PB Max did not last very long—it was discontinued a few years later. Unlike the colas, though, PB Max was a commercial success. Why was it discontinued? According to an anonymous executive cited by Joël Glenn Brenner in his bestselling book *The Emperors of Chocolate*, the Mars family has a distaste for peanut butter and opted to take PB Max out of their product line, despite its substantial contributions to the family's coffers. (This makes sense; Mars's peanut butter M&M's, while common now, are relatively new compared to Reese's Pieces.)

OUTSIDE THE UNION
THE SOVIET FAMILY LOST TO HISTORY

In 1978, a team of Soviet geologists were scanning the Siberian wilderness a hundred miles or so north of the Mongolian border. The area was an undeveloped wilderness—no roads, no electricity, no reservoirs or running water. Like most of Siberia, it was also uninhabited. Which made the geologists' discovery rather unexpected. While flying above the taiga, they saw, below them, a house.

An inhabited house.

During the reign of Peter the Great, a group of fundamentalist members of the Russian Orthodox Church known as Old Believers were oppressed by the tsarist government. Many fled eastward to the edges of Siberia, hoping that isolation would buy them a respite from persecution. For two centuries, this worked well, but when the Bolsheviks took power, the few remaining Old Believers scattered, many going to Bolivia.

However, one family pressed further into Siberia. They were the people discovered by the helicopter pilot scanning the landscape below. Living in a ramshackle, hand-built wooden house was a family of five—a father and four children—and they had been there a long, long time. In 1936, Karp Lykov, his wife, Akulina, and their two children, Savin and Natalia, fled after Karp's brother was killed by Communists. They began a new life for themselves in the middle of nowhere. Akulina gave birth to two more children, son Dmitri and daughter Agafia, in the 1940s (yes, while alone in the taiga).

The family survived on a diet mostly consisting of pine nuts, wild berries, and some rye and potatoes harvested from what they brought with them, but those were meager even during good times. In the 1950s and into the early 1960s, weather and wildlife seemed to conspire against the Lykovs, and they endured a famine. Akulina died from starvation in 1961. Incredibly, all four children were literate and relatively knowledgeable about the outside world. They even knew how to write; as *Smithsonian* magazine reported, their mother taught them the skill "using sharpened birch sticks dipped into honeysuckle juice as pen and ink."

The Lykovs lasted four decades in the wilderness before encountering another human being. While most of the world was struggling with war in Europe, the Lykovs were entirely unaware of the deaths of millions of their countrymen and others. They knew nothing of the Cold War, the Space Race, or of the other scientific, cultural, or political changes throughout the Soviet Union. Karp did, however, show a surprisingly strong appreciation for how technology had advanced. He noticed in the heavens something he attributed to people sending star-like fires into space. What he actually saw were satellites moving across the evening sky.

After being discovered by the geologists in 1978, the Lykovs decided to accept some assistance from the outside world but otherwise chose to remain in their log cabin more than 100 miles away from another human home. In 1981, three of the children—Dmitri, Savin, and Natalia—died from unrelated causes, leaving Karp and his daughter Agafila. Karp passed in 1988, then in his late eighties. Agafila, as of 2013, lives alone, still at the only home she's ever known.

BONUS FACT

Peter the Great really hated beards, seeing them as a throwback to Russia's antiquated history. His solution: a beard tax. Pay it, and you got to keep your beard; otherwise, you had to shave. To help enforce the tax, bearded men (who paid up) were issued a coin as a receipt, which unshaven men had to produce to avoid further fines and harassments. But the tax was short-lived—it proved unpopular and resulted in riots as many refused to either pay or shave.

THE HOLLOW NICKEL
THE SPY WHO CAUGHT HIMSELF

In May 1957, a Finnish man named Reino Häyhänen walked into the United States embassy in Paris. He was there to surrender himself and, ultimately, request amnesty. He was on his way to Moscow but did not want to go there. He claimed he was a Soviet spy and that he was being recalled to the Soviet Union—but he wanted to go back to America, where he had worked as a KGB agent for the previous five years. After U.S. authorities spent a few days checking into his story, he was sent back to the United States. On May 10, 1957, he arrived in New York where he underwent an intense examination by the FBI.

After verifying Häyhänen's identity, the FBI looked to him to solve a puzzle that had been befuddling the agency for four years. According to the Bureau's website (which has a collection of "famous cases and criminals"), one day a newspaper delivery boy discovered a strange-feeling nickel during the course of his daily business. When he dropped it on the ground, the nickel split open. It was hollow. Inside it was a tiny photograph of a list of five-digit numbers. The paperboy, suspecting something fishy (this was the height of the Cold War, after all), brought the coin to the Feds.

The Bureau was baffled. Hollow coins were commonly used by illusionists, but this one was different from anything the FBI or novelty shop owners had seen before. The coin was made from opposite sides of two real coins, somehow connected together. There was a pin-sized hole in front, which the intended recipient could use to pop the halves apart, but the hole was designed to avoid detection and would not have allowed an illusionist easy access to the item held within. Besides, one novelty store shopkeeper told agents, the hollowed-out area was too small for any magic trick. This seemed to be an encoded message, and the intended recipient wasn't the paperboy.

The good news for the FBI? The Bureau, with information given to them by Häyhänen, was able to decode the message. Unfortunately, it wasn't very helpful. It was a letter from the KGB to a Soviet spy who was placed in New York, welcoming him to the United States and explaining some early details of his mission, including where he could get some money to start a new life in America. But it did not help the FBI identify who wrote the note nor its intended recipient.

As it turned out, the G-men didn't have to. Upon further investigation, the FBI declared that it not only knew who the intended recipient was, but it also knew exactly where to find him. In a strange coincidence, the note was intended for Häyhänen himself.

With Häyhänen's continued assistance, the FBI identified a Soviet spy named Rudolf Ivanovich Abel still living in the States. Abel was sentenced to thirty-five years in prison and was ultimately shipped back to Russia in 1962, in exchange for an American pilot who was being held as a prisoner of war.

BONUS FACT

Over a two-week period in 2010, U.S. authorities arrested ten Russian spies. After about ten days, the spies were sent back to Russia in exchange for Americans captured abroad. Why didn't the FBI prosecute instead? According to *Slate*, doing so would require the FBI to disclose, to the courts and therefore the public, the tactics used by these spies. In doing so, the Russian spy agency would know which tactics were no longer viable, and could adjust accordingly. Returning the spies allows the FBI to maintain the secrets to its secrets.

ACOUSTIC KITTY
THE PURR-FECT COLD WAR SPY

For most of the latter half of the twentieth century, the United States and the Soviet Union were leading adversaries in the political and military struggle known as the Cold War. Neither side wanted to overlook a potential advance in technology or espionage, and in the 1960s the CIA found a marriage of the two that could have been a potential game-changer.

That innovation? A bionic spy cat named the Acoustic Kitty.

According to former CIA agent turned author Victor Marchetti, the CIA had developed a way to, literally, wire a cat so that it could be used in espionage missions. The CIA surgically implanted a power supply into the cat, as well as inserting wires going into its brain and its ears. A microphone was layered into its ears and an antenna through its tail. The implanted device was able to determine when the cat was aroused or hungry and suppress those urges, allowing it to carry out its mission—cuddle up to some Soviet officials and listen to their conversations. The entire operation, from start until its end, cost the government somewhere in the ballpark of $20 million and took about five years to develop.

To test Acoustic Kitty, a surveillance van drove up to the test subjects and released the cat, which, again according to Marchetti, made its way across the street unnoticed. Unnoticed, that is, by an oncoming taxi cab, which struck the cat, killing it immediately.

Soon thereafter the CIA decided to drop the spy cat program.

BONUS FACT

In 1995, the United States issued a patent to a pair of Virginia inventors for a "method of exercising a cat." That method, as drafted in patent number 5,443,036, is by playing with the cat with a laser pointer. The patent expired in 2007.

DOGMATIC CATASTROPHES
THE DANGERS OF PET OWNERSHIP

Cats and dogs are popular house pets in the United States. Roughly 35–45 percent of U.S. households own at least one dog (data from several sources varies), and a similar range of households own at least one cat. There are probably well more than 100 million Americans who have a Whiskers or Fido (with hopefully more interesting names) living in their homes, providing affection and companionship.

And an omnipresent source of danger.

When you live with these types of pets, your floors aren't entirely your domain. There's always a chance that your puppy will run through your legs on her way to fetch a ball, that your cat will curl up in the middle of the floor and take a nap, that either will leave a toy or food bowl somewhere other than where it is supposed to be. Foreign objects or four-legged friends hanging out by your feet can lead to stumbles, trips, and in some cases, bad falls.

That's an obvious risk—but how much of one? It may be worse than you'd think.

In the mid-2000s, epidemiologists at the Centers for Disease Control realized that while these pets were "always underfoot," in the words of the lead researcher, Dr. Judy Stevens, no one had tried to quantify the associated dangers. Dr. Stevens and team looked at emergency-room reports from 2001 to 2006. They found that, over the course of that five-year period, more than 86,000 ER visits were due to pets or pet-related causes. That's two visits every hour, twenty-four hours a day, over five years. This number doesn't include less serious injuries that do not require outside medical assistance, at least not immediately, suggesting that the number of everyday, commonplace incidents is significantly higher.

To make matters worse, a disproportionately high number of severe injuries befell the elderly. Most of the injuries were abrasions, contusions, or fractures, but factures were the most severe, constituting nearly 80 percent of the ER visits that resulted in subsequent hospitalization. The highest fracture rates were seen among people aged seventy-five and up. This gave pause to Dr. Harold Herzog, a professor of psychology at Western Carolina University (and a cat owner) who explores the psychological and emotional benefits of pet ownership. He told the *New York Times* "If we were giving a drug that had such a serious side effect, we'd consider taking that drug off the market."

Of course, the CDC didn't recommend anything that drastic. It did, however, suggest increasing public awareness of the dangers—who knew that this book was doing a public service?—and the situations that most likely lead to harm. Because dogs were responsible for 88 percent of the injuries, the CDC further recommended that owners make sure their canine companions receive obedience training as recommended by the American Veterinary Medical Association. The CDC did not go so far as to recommend you should get a cat instead.

BONUS FACT

Goldfish are common household pets—but there's a very common misconception about them. Many people believe that goldfish lack a meaningful long-term memory; some say that a goldfish can only remember the past five seconds of its life. That's not true. Their memory can recall events as far as three months in the past. They can learn to anticipate a meal if you feed them at a regular time each day, and they can be taught to recognize colors, shapes, and sounds.

GOING TO THE DOGS
WHY YOU MAY WANT TO SKIP THE PÂTÉ

You walk into a fancy restaurant and order the pork liver pâté, a high-priced appetizer option at perhaps as much as $10 to $15 for a few forkfuls. It tastes a little funny, perhaps, but you really aren't sure—it's not as if you dine on pâté often enough for your palate to recognize its taste and texture so readily. You enjoy it, though, and rave about the meal to your friends later on.

Even though, for all you know, it may have actually been dog food.

No, there aren't any reports of restaurants making a killing by serving an eighty-eight-cent tin of meat meant for Fido and calling it pâté. But according to a 2009 study published by the American Association of Wine Economists (AAWE), they probably could get away with it.

The three researchers—John Bohannon, Robin Goldstein, and Alexis Herschkowitsch—wanted to see if consumers could recognize the difference between the high-priced stuff one eats at fancy restaurants and the much cheaper stuff you scoop into a dog bowl. To test, they recruited a team of eighteen eaters. Each was informed that they were going to eat dog food. (Yes, they still agreed to participate.) The researchers "assured subjects that the experience would not be disgusting" before they ate the meat samples.

To test, the trio took some Newman's Own Dog Food—it sells for about $2 to $3 per pound—and ran it through a blender to give it the same consistency as pork liver pâté, Spam, liverwurst, and duck liver mousse. The test subjects were asked to sample the five dishes and report on two things:

1. Whether they liked each of the five mystery meats
2. Their guess as to which one was the dog food

The good news: Very few people liked the dog food. Of the eighteen test subjects, thirteen thought it tasted poorly, ranking it last among the options. So there's actually a pretty good reason why restaurants don't serve it, at least to humans—no chef wants to get a reputation for serving poor-tasting pâté.

Then there's the bad news. Only three of the eighteen were able to identify which of the gelatinous gloops on their plates was, in fact, meant for their puppies. One of the eighteen believed the high-priced pâté was the obviously-not-as-expensive dog chow.

As CBS reported, the researchers concluded that "although human beings do not enjoy eating dog food, [we] are also not able to distinguish its flavor profile from other meat-based products that are intended for human consumption."

BONUS FACT

There's another reason why dog food and people food may get mixed up in the future. In April of 2014, ABC News reported that a small pet food company called WeRuVa had developed a line of products marketed as "people food for pets." One of their more notable products, "Kobe Master," uses high-end Kobe-style Wagyu beef as a main ingredient. A thirteen-ounce can sells for $3 to $5.

EGGPLANTS, RICE, DUCK MEAT, AND DOG FOOD
THE INGREDIENTS TO THE WEIRDEST REALITY TV SHOW—EVER

Being an entertainer—a successful one at least—comes with the price of fame. When people know who you are by name, your value as a singer, dancer, actor, or comedian shoots way up. This is probably why there are so many fledgling (and also-ran) entertainers willing to subject themselves to the often humiliating glare of the spotlight on so-called "reality" television shows. At times, it works: Kelly Clarkson, Susan Boyle, and many others have permeated our collective culture via reality television.

In 1998, the opportunity of reality TV knocked on the door of a Japanese comedian named Nasubi. Nasubi (a stage name—his real name is Tomoaki Hamatsu) auditioned for a show in Japan called *Susunu! Denpa Shōnen*, specifically for a segment called (in translation) "Sweepstakes Boy." Nasubi got the part and agreed to the terms: That January, he was to be locked in a small room until he won 1 million yen (roughly $10,000) worth of sweepstakes. In the room was a phone, a chair, lots of pens and postcards so he could enter the sweepstakes, and . . . not much else. No food (although he was probably afforded some supplements), no bed, no toilet paper, and no clothes. As part of the challenge, Nasubi had to strip naked, surrendering his clothes upon entering the room, and the door was then locked behind him. But not all was lost: Nasubi was allowed to use anything he won via the sweepstakes.

The idea, the show producers told Nasubi, was that his life in solitary confinement would be recorded and, if it went well, turned into a television show. This was only partially true. Nasubi's travails were broadcast in weekly highlight shows while he was still in confinement, and within a few months, even that was insufficient. Nasubi's popularity was stunning, so producers broadcast a live feed of his life over the Internet, for all the world to see. He was stark naked except for the image of an eggplant, superimposed over his private parts.

The confinement proved difficult for Nasubi. He did not win anything during the first two weeks, when he scored some jelly—his first real food. A few weeks later, he managed to win a five-pound bag of rice, which he cooked using a tin can, filled with water and placed over his heating unit. He won a television, but because producers did not want him to know that he was on TV, the room did not have a cable or antenna hookup. At one point, he ran out of rice and began to eat dog food, but don't worry: According to the now-defunct website Quirky Japan, a visit to the doctor in May 1998 assessed Nasubi as in good health.

Over time, the winnings piled up. Neatorama reported some highlights:

Two vacuum cleaners . . . four bags of rice, his watermelon, his automobile tires, his belt, and his ladies underwear (the only articles of clothing he won during months of captivity), his four tickets to a Spice Girls movie (which he could not leave his apartment to see), his bike (which he could not ride outside), and countless other items, including chocolates, stuffed animals, headphones, videos, golf balls, a tent, a case of potato chips, a barbecue, and a shipment of duck meat.

In December 1998, Nasubi won another bag of rice, which put him over the 1 million yen threshold. The producers rewarded him with a trip to South Korea, where they immediately stuck him in a new apartment and had him go through the whole thing again, naked, until he won enough in prizes to earn a plane ticket home. He did so three months later.

Upon his return home, the show's producers had one more enclosed room for Nasubi to enter, and he dutifully shed his clothes again and waited for further instruction. Unfortunately, this time, the walls fell to their sides, revealing a naked Nasubi (with no eggplant to shield him) to a crowd of fans who, unbeknownst to him, had been following his every move for months. (He managed to find a pillow to replace the virtual eggplant.) Furthermore, the diary he had been keeping while confined was turned into a very successful book; a video of the ramen noodles he ate after gaining his freedom turned into a commercial; and of course, he was known throughout the country. Nasubi had become a sensation.

BONUS FACT

If you think insane reality TV shows are incredibly popular in Japan, one particular video game makes their ratings seem anemic. That game? *Space Invaders*. Released in 1978, the game was so popular that, according to the book *The Ultimate History of Video Games*, it created a 100-yen coin shortage throughout the country, requiring the Japanese mint to triple production of the coins.

THE MOST FOWL OF PENTHOUSES
THE HOTEL THAT GIVES A QUACK

There's a certain air of elitism that comes with things like red carpets, penthouse suites, processionals, and ornate fountains. We can imagine a movie scene where the leading lady emerges from the palatial top floor of the hotel with all eyes on her. She makes her way down an opulent staircase, draped in deep red, and meets her beau in front of a display of water-spouting cherubs carved from Italian marble. That's typically fantasy, though—made in Hollywood and shipped to the silver screens across the world. However, at the Peabody Hotel in Memphis, Tennessee, such an event is an everyday occurrence.

With one minor change, of course. The Hollywood starlet is anything but. She, and the others who parade down the red carpet, are ducks.

Yes, ducks, as in the waterfowl that quack. Oh, and they're not meeting their dinner dates. The ducks are going for a swim.

The Peabody Hotel Duck March is a daily tradition dating back decades. In the 1930s, the hotel's general manager, Frank Schutt, and a friend went duck hunting in Arkansas but came up empty. Then, as now, duck hunters used decoys to attract potential targets. While modern duck hunters use wooden (i.e., fake) ducks as decoys, back when Schutt and his friend went hunting, it was still acceptable to use live ones. So when they returned to Memphis without having killed any ducks, they weren't entirely empty-handed—they still had the live decoy ducks with them. According to the Peabody Hotel's website, they also were a little too friendly with some Jack Daniel's whiskey, which explains why they thought it'd be funny to let their live ducks go for a swim in the hotel's very expensive fountain made from a solid piece of Italian marble.

Thankfully, the guests appreciated the humor and the cuter-than-typical creatures splashing away. The hotel's owners agreed and decided that ducks should be a permanent addition to the fountain. Of course, if you're going to be silly, you as might as well do it in a big, ostentatious way. The hotel constructed a home for the ducks—called the "Royal Duck Palace"—as part of the hotel's penthouse. And every day at 11 A.M., the hotel rolls out the red carpet for the ducks—literally. The ducks are led from their palace down the temporarily red-clad stairs and into the water as guests watch and applaud. Often, a celebrity is invited to be the marshal of the duck parade, leading the special guests as they make their way to the water.

While you'll find ducks in the fountain at the Peabody, you won't find them on the menu at any of the hotel's restaurants. The Peabody stopped serving the cousins of their guests in 1981 and claim to be the only place in the United States (if not the world) that features a French restaurant not serving duck.

BONUS FACT

Wooden decoys replaced live ducks in the early part of the twentieth century, and by the 1970s, these painted carvings became popular collectables. There's a surprisingly lucrative market for high-end ones. In early 2007, a wooden duck sold at auction for over $850,000, and later that year, two more in private sales went for more than $1 million apiece.

A QUACKY CHRISTMAS TRADITION

DISNEY'S INVASION OF CHRISTMAS (IN SWEDEN)

On December 19, 1958, had you tuned to ABC in the United States, you would have watched a Disney show titled *From All of Us to All of You*. The forty-five-minute special hosted by Mickey Mouse, Jiminy Cricket, and Tinkerbell featured clips from old Disney footage spliced with new content intended to act as a virtual Christmas card of sorts. The special aired in the United States in various forms in subsequent years through the early 1980s and has rarely been on TV since then. It was once released on VHS and laserdisc (!) but never on DVD. Few Americans today can recall ever seeing a version of the special.

But if you're Swedish? Chances are you've seen it a few times.

In 1959—a year after *From All of Us to All of You* debuted in the States—Disney sent a series of dubbed, localized versions to Scandinavia. Sweden's version is called *Kalle Anka och hans vänner önskar God Jul* ("Donald Duck and His Friends Wish You a Merry Christmas") and it debuted on December 24 of that year. The hour-long adaptation has been shown every year since. At 3 P.M. on Christmas Eve, Swedes can tune in to SVT—Sveriges

Television—and enjoy a strangely dated collection of Disney clips from the 1920s to 1950s.

And every year, millions do exactly that. In 2012, for example, 3.8 million Swedes watched Donald Duck—who is more popular in Sweden than Mickey—quack his way through the iconic Christmas special. In a country of only about 9.5 million people total, that's a huge number of viewers. It's enough to make it the second-most watched show in the nation for the entire year, an honor the special has held for four straight years and for the seventh time in ten years. (The other three years? Two third-place finishes and one fourth.)

Watching the show is not simply tradition—it's sacrosanct. In the 1970s, the television station at the time, TV1, considered canceling the special, but upset viewers came out in droves to demand that Donald Duck grace their screens that Christmas. Even tiny changes are not tolerated. As *Slate* reported, in 1982 the show's producers decided to swap out a short titled "Ferdinand the Bull" (which received an Academy Award in 1938) for "The Ugly Duckling." Viewers were enraged, and the next year, the bull was back in its place in Donald's wintertime special. And don't even think about watching it on your DVR—Swedes tune in, live, as if Santa himself were coming down the chimney with Donald.

The reasons for this cultural peculiarity are unclear—some attribute it to timing, as TV first emerged in the Swedish mainstream at the end of the 1950s and early 1960s—but in any event, Christmas duck has a very different meaning in Sweden than it does everywhere else.

BONUS FACT

In an effort to raise money for war bonds during World War II, Walt Disney produced an animated short called *Der Fuehrer's Face*. The short features Donald Duck as a Nazi factory worker whose job it is to screw caps onto artillery shells. Donald's experience as a Nazi worker becomes progressively worse and worse (and more and more ridiculous) until the end—let's not spoil it, as you can usually find the clip on YouTube. Suffice it to say that Donald was always loyal to the Allied cause. The short won an Academy Award for Animated Short Film. It is the only Donald Duck animation to win an Oscar.

HERE COMES SANTA CLAUS
WHY THE U.S. GOVERNMENT TRACKS SANTA'S MOVEMENTS

Every Christmas Eve, children around the world wait for a visitor to arrive through the chimney via reindeer-drawn sleigh, or whatever other means of entry and travel local custom dictates. Santa exists in the hearts and minds of these children. And they like to keep tabs on the jolly man in the red suit. They write him letters at his North Pole address starting in November or December, of course, but there's more that they can do. Since Christmas Eve 1955, children call up the United States military to ask for his current location because the North American Aerospace Defense Command (NORAD), headquartered in Colorado, tracks St. Nick's every move that night. They now have a website, *www.noradsanta.org*, set up for the event, and even make faux videos of Santa delivering gifts on his tour around the globe.

Even though the "tracking" is only slightly more real than Santa himself, this seems like a strange use of multibillion-dollar defense technology and associated personnel. After all, NORAD was a Cold War creation, aimed at defending the U.S. and Canadian airspace from Soviets, not Santas. How did it get in the business of tracking reindeer? Easily: just start with a typo, and add a military officer with a good sense for making kids smile.

On Christmas Eve 1955, Sears ran an advertisement in a newspaper in Colorado Springs, Colorado. The advertisement invited children to call Santa, "direct," on his "private phone," "any time, day or night." Many children took up the invitation, the first one being a young girl.

The man on the other end of the phone wasn't clad in red. The phone, however, was. The phone number in the advertisement was incorrect, and instead of calling the Sears Santa Hotline, as Mentalfloss reports, the child had called a phone at NORAD— and not just any phone. The number led to a red emergency phone typically reserved for incoming messages from the Pentagon or other higher-ups in the military.

The colonel in charge, Harry Shoup—once he figured out that it was a wrong number and not a prank—played along. He told the young caller that he was, indeed, Santa (sometimes it's okay when members of the military lie to citizens) and asked her if she had been good. The two spoke a bit further—about cookies and reindeer, of course—and then Santa Shoup and the girl both hung up.

Then the phone rang again. It was—again—not the Pentagon.

Shoup took the initiative and assigned others to man the phone, speaking to the callers as Santa. The goodwill gesture resonated throughout NORAD's halls and became an annual tradition. Every year, hundreds of volunteers man the phones (and now, e-mail), answering when children call. According to the *Huffington Post*, volunteers are given an "11-page playbook [that] includes a list of nearly 20 questions and answers, including how old is Santa (at least 16 centuries) and has Santa ever crashed into anything (no)."

BONUS FACT

Want to write a letter to Santa? You can—and you'll probably get a reply. After receiving a lot of letters for the jolly man in the red suit in 1974, members of Canada Post's Montreal office decided to write back, hoping to keep children from being disappointed. In 1983, Canada Post took the program national, establishing a program to reply to all letters addressed to Santa. To streamline the process—which, given the million-letter volume, is necessary—Canada Post set up a special mailing address. You can write to St. Nick at "Santa Claus, the North Pole, Canada," with postal code H0H 0H0.

SCRAMBLED FIGHTERS
THE AMERICAN JETS SENT OFF
TO FIGHT WORLD WAR III

The Cuban Missile Crisis began on October 14, 1962, when the United States obtained photographic evidence of a Soviet nuclear missile installation in Cuba. For nearly two weeks, the world was on the brink of nuclear war. The U.S. military went to high alert. Any action on either side of the conflict could have resulted in mutually assured destruction, as both militaries and their nuclear arsenal were at the ready.

On the night of October 25 and into the next morning, that nearly happened. Nuclear-armed U.S. jet planes were ordered to the skies to intercept incoming Soviet bombers. They thought the Soviet Union had started World War III.

Late that evening, around midnight, a would-be intruder attempted to gain access to a military base in Duluth, Minnesota. The base was one of a handful that held a large computer network called the SAGE system—Semi-Automatic Ground Environment— which collected and reconciled radar data to give military officials a single image of the region's airspace. Using this information, officials could coordinate a response in case of a Soviet air assault. Had the Soviets gained access to the Duluth base and sabotaged the computer network, parts of the U.S. military operations would be flying blind.

The intruder did not make it into the Duluth base. A sentry noticed him climbing the fence and shot him, incapacitating the apparent Soviet saboteur. For reasons unreported—given the global situation at the time, this was prudent—the guard sounded the alarm signaling a sabotage attempt. The alarm system was designed to sound in bases throughout the region if not the entire United States—after all, if the Soviets were taking a crack at one base, there's a good chance others were immediately at risk as well. If things went right, many U.S. bases would, once the alarm sounded, run a security sweep for possible breaches.

Unfortunately, things went wrong. At Volk Field in Wisconsin, something was amiss with the alarm wiring. The alarm that sounded wasn't the one signaling a possible saboteur. Instead, it was the one telling nuclear-armed jet fighters to take to the skies. This wasn't a drill, either—the policies at the time did not allow for such practice runs when on such high alert, as to avoid ambiguity. As far as Volk Field's personnel believed, World War III had begun. To make matters worse, because of the activity in Cuba, the military had sent nuclear bombers into patrol, some near Volk Field. Had the interceptors ever taken flight, there's a good chance the American fighters would have shot down their own nuke-laden bombers— and above U.S. soil.

The planes, however, never took off. An official raced from the command center to the runway, probably while the jet fighters were still doing their pre-flight checks, to inform them that it was a false alarm. Not only had the wrong alarm sounded at Volk Field, but there was no saboteur in the first place. The man who tried to invade the Duluth base wasn't a saboteur or a Soviet, or for that matter, a man.

It was a bear.

BONUS FACT

In 2008, a beekeeper in Macedonia noticed that his hives were being attacked by an unknown invader. The culprit, taking a page from Winnie the Pooh's playbook, turned out to be a bear looking for honey. The beekeeper, though, wanted to be compensated for the bear's damage, so the local government pressed criminal charges against the bear, according to the BBC. The bear was convicted in abstentia (officials couldn't locate the bear to arrest him). Because the animal had no owner, the beekeeper was able to collect damages from the local government, totaling about $3,500.

GETTING A HANDLE ON THE PROBLEM

WHY DOORKNOBS ARE BEING BANNED— EXCEPT IN PART OF COLORADO

In 1999, the U.S. Small Business Administration and the Department of Justice teamed up to provide a guide for small businesses, helping them comply with the requirements of the Americans with Disabilities Act (ADA). Among the suggestions is a subsection dealing with "architectural barriers"—"physical features that limit or prevent people with disabilities from obtaining the goods or services that are offered." Of specific note are round doorknobs, as they may be difficult for some people to grip and turn, thereby preventing access to whatever's on the other side. In late 2013, Vancouver (Canada) echoed its neighbors to the south and banned round knobs on doors on any new housing built within its borders. If you want to respect those who are differently abled, you may want to go with lever-like handles instead. As *Popular Science* argued, they're "the way of the future."

Just don't tell that to the people of Aspen, Colorado. Because in many parts of that area, not only are round doorknobs allowed; they're required by law.

The reason? Bears.

Aspen is the largest town in Pitkin County, with just under 9,000 full-time residents. That constitutes roughly half of the county's population—but only if you count people. Due to the large amount of forest in the area, Pitkin County is also home to 5,000–10,000 black bears.

The bears eat about 20,000 calories a day during the summer and autumn months as they prepare for hibernation, and when it comes to a meal, they're not all that picky. Often, a bear will wander into town in search of food, and let's face it, we humans do a great job of leaving snacks out. Unsecured garbage cans, uncleaned barbecues, and birdfeeders are specifically mentioned by the Aspen authorities as open invitations to a foraging bear. In fact, from April 15 to November 15—that's bear season—a city ordinance specifically prohibits residents from using birdfeeders.

As of the summer of 2010, doorknobs also fell under a bear-control ordinance. There were a few instances of bears entering people's homes and businesses, not understanding that it was inappropriate to do so; bears shouldn't be expected to know that breaking and entering is both illegal and impolite. Levers, as the ADA compliance guide notes, are easier to open for people who can't grip and turn things. Bears lack opposable thumbs and, therefore, find levers much easier to open than they do the classic doorknob. So the Pitkin County government, as the Sky-Hi News reported, passed a law that "requires solid, round-handled doorknobs rather than the lever variety on exterior doors on all new homes" in the areas near bear habitats.

The rule had its skeptics and dissenters, of course. Some saw it as governmental overreach, while others pointed out that the bears could often flatten the knobs or just smash down doors. (They're bears, after all.) But don't worry about any issues regarding ADA compliance. The Sky-Hi News assures that "exemptions are made for doors that must meet disability standards."

BONUS FACT

Ever notice that many doorknobs are made of brass or copper? There's a reason for that. Those types of metals are poisonous to many types of household germs (although we don't yet have a good explanation as to why), and doorknobs made of those materials disinfect themselves slowly over the course of about eight hours.

BEARING ARMS
POLAND'S UNLIKELY WORLD WAR II HERO

In January of 1944, Europe was in the throes of war, and seemingly nothing (save perhaps for Switzerland) was beyond its theater. About eighty miles outside of Rome was the abbey of Monte Cassino, a monastery dating back to 529. The Germans decided to not occupy the abbey in spite of its tactical value—it was placed on top of a hill and made an excellent location for lookouts—likely in deference to its history. However, American intelligence erroneously determined otherwise and the air force bombed the abbey, reducing it to ruins. German soldiers then paratrooped in, and for the four months that followed, Allied and Axis battled over the region. All together, the two sides suffered casualties numbering as high as 75,000; the Allies ultimately prevailed.

But the Battle of Monte Cassino is not only known for its relatively high casualty count or the American intelligence failure. Another hallmark of the battle was the diversity of Allied troops who fought there. There were soldiers from the United States, Great Britain, the French Underground, New Zealand, Canada, British India, Poland, some anti-Mussolini Italians, and even an Iranian. The Iranian's name was Wojtek.

Wojtek was a bear.

(Yes, an actual bear.)

Wojtek was discovered by a local Iranian boy in 1942 when he was just a cub. The boy sold him to a group of men in the Polish Army who were engaged in battle in the region—apparently, the soldiers wanted a pet/mascot, and the boy wanted some of their rations. Wojtek quickly became one of the boys, even taking up cigarettes, according to the *Scotsman*. (Wojtek did not just smoke them—he also ate them.) As his company moved throughout the Middle East, Wojtek became increasingly popular with the troops, but when British ships came to move the Polish Army into Italy, only enlisted men and officers were allowed on board. So the Polish Army did what seemed at the time to make sense to someone: They drafted Wojtek into service. He joined as a private in the 22nd Artillery Supply Company of the Polish II Corps.

As a private, Wojtek was no longer just a marmalade-loving curiosity—he had to live in the tents with his fellow enlisted men and, when duty called, press into battle. Being a bear, there were few jobs he could do. (Even if he were a super-intelligent bear—and there was no evidence that he was—he could not, for example, shoot a rifle, as bears lack opposable thumbs.) However, as legend has it, he actually did something useful during the Battle of Monte Cassino. Private Wojtek acted as a transport—moving heavy crates of artillery from the supply lines to the weapons. According to the witnesses who swear that it happened, Wojtek did so perfectly, never dropping a single crate.

After the war, Wojtek found a permanent home in the Edinburgh Zoo. It became customary for Polish soldiers to visit him and, when they did, to toss him a cigarette—which Wojtek would then smoke. He lived to be twenty-two years old, finally passing on in 1963. To date, he's the world's only known war hero who happens to be a bear.

BONUS FACT

American icon Smokey Bear was created in 1944 by the U.S. Forestry Service to educate the public about the dangers of forest fires (and how to prevent them from occurring). By 1964, Smokey was receiving so much fan mail that the U.S. Postal Service issued him his own ZIP code. It's 20252.

FLUSHED AWAY
WHAT GOES DOWN MUST COME UP

Reflecting back on World War II, British Prime Minister Winston Churchill once wrote that "the only thing that really frightened me during the war was the U-boat peril." U-boats—the German submarine fleet—patrolled the Atlantic throughout the war, wreaking havoc on Allied convoys carrying troops, supplies, and everything else flowing between the United States and Western Europe. Over the course of the war, German forces sank nearly 4,000 ships and took the lives of roughly 75,000 sailors and merchant marines, in no small part due to the advantages gained by this submarine fleet.

Over time, Allied forces developed different ways to detect and, ultimately, destroy these subs. On April 14, 1945, the British managed to sink one of the U-boats without any technological advantages—at least not on the Allies' part—shortly after it surfaced just off the shores of Scotland.

Why would the U-boat surface there? The crew didn't have a choice.

Someone flushed the toilet when he shouldn't have.

That's not a euphemism for a screwup, either—that's quite literally what happened. This U-boat was a very new one—it was on its first (and last) patrol—and it had some new features. For example, *U-1206* was outfitted with a special type of toilet that allowed the men on board to hit the head while the submarine was well below the ocean's surface. This wasn't a simple "do your business and pull the chain" toilet. Operating it—that is, flushing it—required training, and not everyone on the U-boat had been so educated. Those who availed themselves of these toilets during deep-sea dives needed to call in one of these specifically trained toilet flushers to finish the job. Apparently, someone forgot that step.

The errant flush caused a leak and water entered the U-boat's batteries, which, according to *Wired*, were located beneath the toilet. The waterlogged batteries began to emit chlorine gas, which is toxic. So the U-boat's crew, facing near-certain death if they stayed at dive depth, surfaced to air everything out.

Before the crew could fix the problem and clear out the toxic fumes, the ship was detected by the British and, shortly thereafter, sunk by the Royal Air Force. Four men aboard were killed, the other forty-six captured by the British, and *U-1206* was destined for an eternity at the bottom of the North Sea, its super-toilets submerged under 200 meters of water.

BONUS FACT

More than three dozen nations (through 2013) now have submarine fleets. If one were to rank the fleets by the number of subs, Russia, China, and the United States would be in the top four, which makes sense given the respective size of their nations, economies, and militaries. But none of them are atop the list. Number one? Perhaps surprisingly, it is North Korea.

MAN NOT OVERBOARD
WHY WOMEN AND CHILDREN GO FIRST

The apex of chivalry—at least, in the romanticized sense of the word—occurs on a boat destined for the bottom of the ocean. "Women and children first" is the rallying cry—the idea being that lifeboats should go to them first, and that men, like the captain, should go down with the ship if need be. The ritual is so ingrained in our culture that we almost expect it as a plot element in any story, fiction or nonfiction, involving such a disaster. But where did it come from?

In 1852, a British frigate, HMS *Birkenhead*, was charged with transporting troops from England and Ireland to South Africa as part of a decades-long military campaign against the native peoples, called the Xhosa Wars. Also on board were the wives and families of many of the officers; they were allowed to stay with their husbands while the men were stationed overseas. But the *Birkenhead* would never arrive at her intended destination. While making her way around Western Cape, the South African province that calls Cape Town its capital, the *Birkenhead* hit a submerged, uncharted rock and began to take on water. The captain ordered the soldiers on board to help pump the ship dry, but it soon became clear that the *Birkenhead* was doomed to plummet to the ocean's bottom. The captain changed his order. Everyone who was able to swim was to jump overboard and make it to lifeboats now in the water. Everyone—man, woman, and child alike. Even the nine cavalry horses being transported were blindfolded and cajoled overboard, in hopes that they could make the two-mile swim to shore.

But for the soldiers, the captain's order was subordinate to that of their commanding officer, Lieutenant-Colonel Alexander Seton. Seton, likely fearing that a mad rush to safety would cause further harm (and put lifeboats at risk), ordered his men to stand pat, allowing the women and children to take to the boats. Almost all the soldiers followed the order and stood on the ship, likely dooming themselves to death, as the *Birkenhead* broke up into the cold ocean water surrounding its shattering hull. Of the 640 or so people aboard the *Birkenhead* (we don't have an exact number because the records sank with the ship), just under 200 survived, most of them women and children. (Oh, and eight of the nine horses managed to survive, too, in case you were wondering.)

The idea that women and children should be allowed to evacuate first became a maritime practice soon after, but the phrase "women and children first!" did not enter naval parlance for almost a decade. By the time the HMS *Titanic* sank in 1912, the custom was well established. Nearly 75 percent of the women and more than 50 percent of the children aboard the doomed ship survived, compared to only 20 percent of the men.

BONUS FACT

The Xhosa Wars are named after the Xhosa, indigenous people in South Africa who resisted British imperialism. In 1856, a teenage Xhosa girl named Nongqawuse went to the cattle fields to scare away birds. While there, she'd later say, she was visited by three spirits. They told her that to triumph over the British settlers, the Xhosa needed to kill all their cattle and raze all their crops. The prophecy made its way to the chief of Nongqawuse's clan, who believed that the visions were real and ordered the slaying of an estimated 300,000 cattle. This resulted in a massive famine among the Xhosa, resulting in the death of roughly 40,000 of their people.

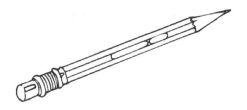

THE PENCIL TEST
HOW WOOD PLUS GRAPHITE EQUALED RACISM

From the 1940s until 1994, South Africa was an apartheid state—people were classified based on their race, with whites having rights that were denied to blacks. But "white" and "black" wasn't the end of the classification system. Mixed-race people—called "coloureds"—were considered a class unto themselves. While black people were discriminated against in almost all aspects of life, mixed-raced people were generally afforded more rights than blacks—yet were hardly considered equal to whites.

"Mixed-race" isn't an easily defined class. How many white grandparents or great-grandparents does one need to be considered "white"? Or "mixed-race"? Apart from the fact that we shouldn't be classifying people in such a manner anyway, trying to answer that question is an impossible task that can only lead to absurd results. So it should surprise no one that South Africa's system involved something both outlandish and offensive, called the pencil test.

The pencil test, as Wikipedia explains, was a "method of assessing whether a person has Afro-textured hair." A pencil was inserted into the person's hair and that person's racial category was determined by how easily it came out. If the pencil fell out, the testee was considered white. If the pencil stuck, then the person was ruled non-white. Black people could subject themselves to the test in hopes of being reclassified as coloured. In such a case, after the pencil was inserted into the person's hair, he or she was told to shake his or her head. If the pencil fell out, the person was from that point on considered coloured; otherwise, he or she remained black.

The test led to absurd results, even accounting for the bigoted nature of its purpose. Of particular note was the case of Sandra Laing, a darker-skinned girl born to two white parents (and from at least three generations of white ancestors). In the mid-1960s, Laing, then ten years old, was subjected to the pencil test to determine the "true" nature of her race. When the pencil remained lodged in her hair, she was ruled to be coloured and, therefore, expelled from her (all-white) school. Despite her father's insistence that Sandra was his daughter and the results of a paternity test supporting his assertion, the Laings were thereafter considered outcasts from the white community.

The pencil test lasted well into the 1990s, only officially falling onto the ash heap of South African history when the apartheid regime crumbled in 1994.

BONUS FACT

How did South Africa handle people of Asian descent? Depends on one's nationality. In the 1960s, Japanese people were considered "honorary whites," likely in an effort to encourage trade between the two nations, as whites in South Africa were not allowed to otherwise associate with non-whites. However, most other Asian groups were not offered the same classification until years later. Chinese people, for example, were not considered "honorary whites" until 1984.

SHARPEN FOR DRUGS
THE PENCIL WITH THE UNFORTUNATE MESSAGE

The American "War on Drugs" began informally in the early 1970s. On October 27, 1970, Congress passed the Comprehensive Drug Abuse Prevention and Control Act, and the next year, two members of the legislative body issued a report asserting that 10–15 percent of servicemen in Vietnam were heroin addicts. In response, President Richard Nixon declared in a press conference that drug abuse was "public enemy number one in the United States"—and presidents and politicians since, by and large, have followed suit.

While punishment and treatment are the hallmarks of the War on Drugs, anti-drug messaging has also been a major component, especially as it pertains to children and teens. Countless public service announcements, posters, and other media have been put toward this effort. In the late 1990s, one group tried a new method of messaging—custom imprinting slogans on the sides of the ubiquitous Number 2 pencils used throughout schools.

The idea seemed like an easy one: print the words "Too Cool to Do Drugs" on the pencils, turning each ten-cent writing utensil into an anti-drug nudge.

But then the kids started to use them. The pencils, that is, not drugs.

To use a Number 2 pencil, you have to sharpen it. And the more you sharpen it, the more the pencil shrinks, sometimes down to just a point attached to that little metal sleeve that holds the little pink eraser. Normally, that's not an issue. In this case, though, it was a particularly egregious problem. The words were positioned in such a way that, as children used their pencils, the message changed. "Too Cool to Do Drugs" soon became "Cool to Do Drugs" and, not long after, simply "Do Drugs."

The organization that sponsored the special pencils, the Bureau for At-Risk Kids, recalled them after a ten-year-old at a New York–area school noticed the problem. The bureau ended up re-issuing the pencils with the message repositioned so that it shortened, when the pencil was sharpened, to read "Too Cool." But if you really want one that's not "Too Cool" and advocates for drug use instead, you can find them online pretty easily.

BONUS FACT

The little metal sleeve that attaches the eraser to the rest of a Number 2 pencil? It has a name—it's called a ferrule.

TOBACCO TO SCHOOL
THE UNLIKELY SPONSORS OF SOME CHINESE ELEMENTARY SCHOOLS

On May 12, 2008, an 8.0 magnitude earthquake struck Sichuan, China. The earthquake and its aftershocks took the lives of nearly 70,000 people with another 20,000 deemed missing. An additional 375,000 people were injured. The region's infrastructure was also badly damaged—estimates vary, but between 5 and 10 million people lost their homes, constituting perhaps as much as 50 percent of the area's population. In hopes of rebuilding the region, the Chinese government set aside the equivalent of nearly $150 billion, a huge amount of money, but probably much less than what was needed to return Sichuan back to its former state. Many private businesses rose to the occasion, finding funding and solutions for those affected by the tragedy.

That is why some children in the area go to the Tobacco Hope Elementary School.

After the earthquake, tobacco companies were on the forefront of the effort to revitalize education in the region. The China Tobacco Company—working with an organization called Project Hope—opened seventy schools over the course of a year throughout the region. In exchange, the tobacco industry bought sponsorship rights. Schools come with textbooks, desks, pencil sharpeners, and a side of pro-nicotine propaganda; one school, by way of example, had the message "Work hard for society! Tobacco can help you become an achiever!" on its walls.

The move was, of course, controversial. According to a survey by Peking University, nearly one-third of boys under the age of fifteen had tried a cigarette at least once. (Less than 10 percent of similarly-aged American children have lit up.) Among smokers, the average age of their first cigarette was ten. In hopes of stemming the tide, tobacco advertisements are banned from newspapers, TV, and radio in China—so one would think that the walls of schools would be treated similarly if not more stringently.

The tobacco industry wasn't shirking from criticism. A spokesperson for the China Tobacco Company told *Beijing Today* that the company was just doing its part to help the region recover from disaster: "Tobacco firms should not be barred from contributing to social welfare simply because the cigarettes they produce are harmful to their user's health." For low-income areas, finding the 200,000 yuan (about $30,000 to $35,000) to open a Project Hope school was an otherwise impossible task, as no other sponsors popped up.

For the time being, the tobacco lobby isn't stopping these sponsorships. Through 2011, they've helped open more than 100 schools as well as a network of libraries. Parents whose children use these resources seem okay with the arrangement. Wu Yiqun, a researcher and opponent of the tobacco-branded schools, told the *Telegraph* that "parents are actually very supportive of the tobacco companies. They think they are giving something back to society." But Wu, who also noted that schools give out cigarette-shaped candy, cautioned that the tobacco companies "are just using charity as a front."

BONUS FACT

In the United States, the American Legacy Foundation runs a lot of anti-smoking ads. The Foundation's main source of income? The tobacco companies themselves. In 1998, four major tobacco companies entered into a settlement with the attorneys general of forty-six states; the settlement, among other things, called for creation of an anti-smoking media entity funded by annual payments from the cigarette companies.

PANDA DIPLOMACY
CHINA'S VERY CUTE AND LUCRATIVE ANIMAL RENTAL BUSINESS

On August 23, 2013, a giant panda named Mei Xiang gave birth to a cub at the National Zoo in Washington, DC, grabbing the world's attention. Giant pandas are an endangered species, with only a few hundred living in captivity and an estimated 2,000 to 3,000 living in the wild. Most of the giant pandas in captivity (and all of the ones in the wild) are in China, but if you'd like to see one elsewhere, many zoos across the world have a few. In the United States the National Zoo now has three, Zoo Atlanta has four, and the San Diego Zoo has two. There are also giant pandas in zoos in Canada, Mexico, Austria, Spain, Australia, Singapore, and a half dozen or so other countries.

However, the pandas don't really live there—at least not permanently. They're all on vacation of sorts. Mei Xiang and the others are owned by China and are participating in a lucrative panda-lending program.

Originally, China gave pandas to countries—no strings attached. Starting in the 1950s, the Chinese government used the popularity (and adorableness) of giant pandas to curry favor with other nations by gifting the creatures to governments around the world. In 1972, for example, China gave two giant pandas to the United States as thanks for President Richard Nixon's historic visit to their nation (which itself began to normalize the relationship between the two countries). First Lady Pat Nixon ensured that those two pandas, Ling-Ling and Hsing-Hsing, were housed at the National Zoo. The program was very successful. Other countries—many of which had little in the way of relations with China—asked for pandas as well. In 1984, though, China stopped giving pandas away. Instead, the Chinese government began loaning them out.

Under the terms of the revised Chinese plan, zoos were offered pandas only for a ten-year period. (There's some evidence that renewals are possible.) Because all the pandas now in captivity outside of China were born after the 1984 change, "all giant pandas outside China are actually on loan from the country," as NPR points out. The cost of renting a panda is $1,000,000 per year, payable to China's Wildlife Conservation Association. Perhaps most strikingly, the lease agreement requires that any cubs born to loaned-out pandas be returned to China. So Mei Xiang's addition will likely go back to China at some point early on in its life. The good news, though, is that the baby will be reunited with its brother. Tai Shan, a panda born to Mei Xiang in 2005, was returned to China in 2009.

BONUS FACT

How do pandas go from China to points abroad, and back? They fly FedEx, pursuant to a special deal between the air-freight hauler and the Chinese government. The plane used has a big picture of a panda eating leaves painted on the side, and the pandas themselves fly in a crate with transparent side walls.

THE MADMAN IN THE WHITE HOUSE
RICHARD NIXON'S CRAZY THEORY ON PREVENTING A NUCLEAR WAR

For most of the Cold War, three words dictated the game theory outcomes behind military strategies: mutually assured destruction. At any moment, the United States and its NATO allies could volley nuclear missiles at the Soviet Union, destroying the Russians in the process. The Soviets, however, could do the same to the Western powers. If either side acted, the other would have ample time to react. Who shot first would hardly matter, as in the end, we'd all suffer the same fate.

Which is exactly what Richard Nixon counted on.

On October 10, 1969, the United States military was ordered to prepare for war. As the *Boston Globe* would recount three and a half decades later, "nuclear armed fighter planes were dispersed to civilian airports, missile countdown procedures were initiated, missile-bearing submarines were dispersed, long-range bombers were launched, targeting was begun." The American military was ready to start World War III.

But if America was about to defeat the Communists, it didn't make headlines; the country was more interested in the New York Mets' ultimate triumph over the Baltimore Orioles in the World

Series. The average citizen had little knowledge of the ramp-up to war. The same could be said for the servicemen involved, for that matter. Very little context, if any, was provided—America was not provoked in any meaningful way leading up to the readiness alert, and no rationale for this upsurge in activity made its way down the chain of command.

And then, things got even crazier. On October 27, the U.S. Strategic Air Command dispatched bombers armed with thermonuclear warheads, ordering them to fly over Alaska and toward the Soviet Union. For three days, the bombers circled around the Arctic, just out of Soviet airspace, awaiting further instruction. Stateside, few people—and nearly no civilians—had any idea this was going on. But it certainly caught the attention of the powers-that-be in Moscow.

Nixon's gambit was an attempt to make the Soviet Union think he was crazy. His strategy, later termed the "madman theory," was based on the idea that even the slightest provocation by the Soviets would result in Nixon blowing a figurative gasket, tossing nukes at the USSR as a sign of American strength, and not really giving a you-know-what about the consequences. The Soviets could be convinced of his own irrationality, Nixon surmised, and the odds of Soviet aggression would be greatly reduced.

It is unlikely that the "madman theory" ended up paying dividends. For much of 1969, the Soviet Union and China were engaged in a border dispute, a culmination of the ongoing deterioration of Soviet and Chinese relations. While the incipient conflict wound down in September of that year, negotiations over the delineation of the two nations' borders again heated up at around the same time Nixon feigned madness. More likely than not, Soviet leadership saw America's bombers not as the evidence of insanity that Nixon hoped, but rather that of a strategic decision to support China in case the two Communist nations went to war.

BONUS FACT

Lyndon Baines Johnson occupied the White House just before Richard Nixon did, and LBJ may have had the better resume when it came to faking people out. According to the National Park Service, LBJ would drive guests around in his blue car and, while rolling down a hill toward a lake, scream that the brakes were out and that he and his passengers were about to be in big trouble. But the joke was on his guests—the blue car was an Amphicar, a German-made amphibious automobile designed to float on the water's surface.

COLD WATER WAR
THE COMMUNIST SKIRMISH THAT TOOK PLACE IN A SWIMMING POOL

In 1958, Mao Zedong, then the Chairman of the Chinese Communist Party and the leader of China; and Nikita Khrushchev, the leader of the Communist Party of the Soviet Union, and thus the USSR's *de facto* head of state, gathered for a photo op. It was all smiles, as any such posed photo would be. Behind the scenes, though, things weren't so rosy. While both men were leaders in the Communist world, they had experienced a major ideological rift. After Stalin's death in 1953, Khrushchev was one of the leading voices in favor of more friendly relations with the non-Communist West; he eschewed the Stalinesque cult of personality common to both the USSR and China. Mao, on the other hand, took a much more aggressive approach to relations with the United States and Europe.

Starting in the mid-1950s, the relationship between China and the USSR began to fracture, and the period from 1960 through 1989 is now known as the Sino-Soviet Split, marking the two nations' irreconcilable differences. Being the world's two most important Communists, its leaders at the time put on a good show leading up to that point. The meeting just described was one such moment, but what followed was better—until some details began to emerge.

Mao invited Khrushchev to a pool party.

The discussions between Mao and Khrushchev were focused on joint defensive efforts but went nowhere, quickly, as neither side wished to give in to the other. The tension during the talks gave Mao an idea—ratchet down the hostilities by reducing the formalities. He invited Khrushchev to join him at one of Mao's many palatial homes, and on August 3, 1958, the two met again.

According to *Smithsonian* magazine, on that day, Mao greeted Khrushchev in a bathrobe and slippers. One of Mao's aides presented Khrushchev with a gift—a green bathing suit. Khrushchev and Mao, per the Chinese leader's insistence, were going to cool down their negotiations by cooling down themselves. They were going for a swim in the pool.

That sounds great, except for one big problem—if you're Khrushchev, that is. The Soviet premier knew many things about the world, but how to swim was not one of them. This fact was almost certainly known to Mao beforehand, who likely used the knowledge to embarrass his Soviet counterpart. Mao swam laps while translators ran back and forth, poolside, relaying his words to Khrushchev, who was standing in the shallow end waiting, and almost certainly steaming as well.

Mao wasn't done embarrassing his counterpart, either. He insisted that Khrushchev join him in the deeper water. *Smithsonian* describes the result:

> A flotation device was suddenly produced—Lorenz Lüthi describes it as a "life belt," while Henry Kissinger prefers "water wings." Either way, the result was scarcely dignified. Mao, says Lüthi, covered his head with "a handkerchief with knots at all the corners" and swept up and down the pool while Khrushchev struggled to stay afloat. After considerable exertion, the Soviet leader was able to get

moving, "paddling like a dog" in a desperate attempt to keep up. "It was an unforgettable picture," said his aid Oleg Troyanovsky, "the appearance of two well-fed leaders in swimming trunks, discussing questions of great policy under splashes of water."

Yes, that's right: on the urgency of Mao Zedong, Nikita Khrushchev donned a pair of swimmies—and, a bit more than coincidentally, the two nations' relations were never quite the same.

BONUS FACT

Russia's Vladimir Putin has a reputation for pulling the same sort of stunts as Mao did. In 2006, Putin hosted Germany's Angela Merkel in Moscow for some high-profile negotiations. Also attending were Putin's pet dogs—which were likely invited to give the Russians an upper hand at the table. As *Foreign Policy* reported, Merkel isn't fond of dogs—she was bitten by one as a young child and has avoided them since.

SWIMMING ALONE
THE WHALE WHO HAS NO FRIENDS TO TALK TO

Whales—particularly humpback whales—speak. Their language is not an articulate mix of sounds like the ones we humans make, but some whales, such as the aforementioned humpbacks, make sounds akin to singing. It is widely believed by the relevant scientific communities that these sounds are how members of these species communicate with one another.

Which is why a whale dubbed the 52-hertz whale is, forever, alone.

Most whale sounds occur in the 15- to 25-hertz frequency range. But the 52-hertz whale uniquely (as far as we know) creates a sound at a much higher frequency. Unfortunately for the 52-hertz whale, this massive difference in frequency means that it cannot communicate with the other whales in the ocean.

Scientists at the Woods Hole Oceanographic Institution (WHOI) have been tracking the whale since detecting its strange noise in 1992 using hydrophones, a series of underwater listening devices originally used to track submarine movements. When the team discovered the whale, its members were surprised, to say the least. As reported by the *New York Times*, "its sonic signature is clearly that of a whale, but nothing like the normal voice of the giant blue or the next biggest species, the fin, or any other whale for that matter"; so says a WHOI marine biologist studying the whale. Further, the WHOI team believes that the whale is in otherwise good health, noting that it would be extremely unlikely that a creature with compromised health could live in solitude for over a dozen years—as the 52-hertz whale has.

Its life of solitude is manifested also in its odd migratory pattern. The 52-hertz whale typically travels up and down the Pacific coast of Mexico, the United States, and Canada, venturing into the Gulf of Alaska but not venturing farther north. According to the *Alaska Dispatch*, the gray whale migrates in a similar path, but ventures much farther north to feed; the 52-hertz whale never reaches that feeding ground and is therefore not likely part of that pack. As of January 2012, it was last detected south of Alaska, alone, as usual.

In fact, we don't know what species of whale the 52-hertz is. While some believe it is a species in and of itself—perhaps the last whale of its kind—WHOI believes that is not the case. Rather, the cetologists of WHOI believe it is simply a strange, unique humpback whale.

BONUS FACT

The blue whale is the world's largest animal. It is so large that its tongue alone weighs about three tons (or about 2,700 kilograms). For comparison's sake, the largest land animal, the African bush elephant—the whole thing, not just the tongue—weighs about six tons.

DOWN BY THE BAY
THE STRANGE EFFECT 9/11 HAD ON THE WHALE POPULATION

Canada's Bay of Fundy is located on the East Coast of North America, tucked between Maine, New Brunswick, and Nova Scotia. It's a common home to a number of ships and active ports, at least on a typical day. But September 11, 2001, was not a typical day. The attacks on the United States brought sea traffic throughout the region to a crawl as authorities rushed to ensure the safety of ships, their passengers, and their cargo. That slowdown lasted a couple of days and unintentionally created unique conditions for scientific inquiry.

For example, it helped researchers discover that whales were really stressed out.

The Bay of Fundy is a seasonal feeding ground for a few species of whales, whose populations spike in the summer and into the early fall. As a relatively enclosed body of water, the Bay of Fundy lends itself well to the study of these creatures. In September 2001, two teams of researchers were independently conducting whale-focused experiments in the area. One was collecting recordings of whale songs, to learn more about how whales communicate. The other was collecting whale feces, which, while gross, can be used to tell us more about whale diet and nutrition by measuring various hormone levels found within the stool samples. (The things we do in furtherance of science.)

Nearly a decade after 9/11, a group led by scientists from the New England Aquarium in Boston noticed that these two experiments provided a rare opportunity. For years, as the *New York Times* reported, we've known that whales "communicate with acoustic signals at low frequency, the range of many noises from ships" and that "whales move off, reduce their own calls and otherwise respond to ship noise." Some researchers believed that whales were moving away because ship noise caused them stress, but there was no good way to test this theory. Incredibly, the 9/11 data provided a rare insight into the question.

When whales get stressed, they release a hormone that, ultimately, they excrete in their feces. Because researchers were collecting the poop on 9/11 and the days previous and subsequent, the science community had data on the relative stress levels of the Bay of Fundy whales during that time. What it shows is that the whales were pretty relaxed on the days after the attack—or, at least, more relaxed than they were in the days prior.

From the same time period, we also have data measuring the amount of low-frequency acoustic signals in the Bay that week— again, from before and after 9/11. We already knew that ship traffic came to a near-halt, so it shouldn't be surprising that the amount of underwater noise also dropped dramatically. One could say that it was, relatively speaking, rather peaceful if you were a whale.

Whether the whales' stress levels are important, though, is harder to determine. Since the conditions of this experiment were accidental, researchers can't repeat the tests. One of the researchers pointed out, in the words of the Associated Press, that it is "unclear how much chronic stress from noise the whales can take before the population is affected, largely because it's impossible to conduct controlled experiments on fifty-ton animals." So for now, we'll likely keep stressing out the whales.

BONUS FACT

Life as a college student can be stressful, too, especially around finals. A few schools have found a cute solution—puppies. The schools bring in trained therapy animals to take some of the edge off.

ENJOY THE SILENCE
HOW YOUR CELL PHONE MAKES YOU HAPPIER BY LYING TO YOU

You're on your cell phone, talking about something or other. Suddenly, you realize that the other person is strangely quiet—too quiet. "Still there?" you ask the void, hopelessly, as you already know the answer. The other person didn't just stop talking. Your call has been disconnected.

Again, you knew that already. But *how* did you know that?

The answer: your cell phone provider tricks you. (In a good way, though.)

When we have real, in-person conversations, it is rarely, if ever, in a place of true silence. Perhaps an air conditioner is running or birds are chirping or someone is rustling papers quietly at his or her desk. These tiny background sounds aren't interrupting your conversations, though. Subconsciously, we anticipate them (this is often, in aggregate, called "white noise"), and they act as a signal to our brains that all's normal. However, communications that aren't in person—cell phones and radio, especially—don't have this white noise. Sure, there are the background sounds in the area in which we're standing or sitting, but when the speaker is in another area, that doesn't do us much good.

So we fake it. Or, rather, the cell phone companies do, by adding what is called "comfort noise." Wikipedia defines it as "synthetic background noise used in radio and wireless communications to fill the artificial silence." It's not the easiest thing to provide. All the sounds we hear on our cell phones are just data bits being translated into sound, and transmitting that data takes up bandwidth. This is true for real conversations and comfort noise alike, so many companies are in the business of optimizing this useful static.

And no, eliminating comfort noise isn't an option; that would lead to a surprising number of "hello?"s and "you there?"s. According to one provider of comfort noise, "most conversations include about 50 percent silence."

BONUS FACT

Radio was an incredibly important form of mass communication during World War II. For example, before and after air raids, the city of Leningrad broadcast instructions to take cover, and later would issue the all-clear, over a municipal radio service. That radio system reached most of the city; it had about half a million households and businesses with speakers, and another 10–20,000 loudspeakers on the street. What if the Germans bombed the transmitters? How would the people of Leningrad know? To account for this, the city radio employed an early version of comfort noise, softly broadcasting the sound of a metronome when no announcements were being made.

FEELING BUZZED
WHY WE THINK OUR PHONES ARE VIBRATING—
EVEN THOUGH THEY AREN'T

You're sitting at your desk, standing in the kitchen, watching TV, etc. All of a sudden, your cell phone vibrates, informing you that you have a new text message, phone call, or e-mail. You reach into your pocket and check, only to find no such message—and perhaps you discover that your phone is not even in your pocket. The vibration felt real, but what caused it? Evidently, not your cell phone.

If this has happened to you, rest assured you are not alone.

In 2010, a team of researchers from Baystate Medical Center in Springfield, Massachusetts, asked 232 of their colleagues to answer a questionnaire about phantom vibrations from their cell phones (or, more correctly, from the area where their cell phones usually are). Of the 176 who responded, 115—69 percent—stated that yes, they experienced the disconcerting fake alerts like those just described. The researchers' plain-as-day conclusion: "Phantom-vibration syndrome is common among those who use electronic devices."

What causes it? There are a lot of theories. Discovery News suggested that "[it] could be because cell phones produce electrical signals that transmit the feeling of vibration directly to a person's nerves or simply because of the mental anticipation of alerts." Mental Floss explains one way this might work, likening it to "a physical stimulation similar to what happens when your phone is near a speaker and you hear that weird buzzing sound as it does a 'hand shake' with a cell tower and gives off some electromagnetic interference." The anticipation is not dissimilar from any other sort of psychological conditioning—we are so used to our phones vibrating that our brains make it feel like it is happening when we expect it, not when it actually does.

There's some newer evidence suggesting that these false vibrations are all in our heads. In July 2012, researchers published a study on the phantom-vibration phenomenon after speaking with undergraduate students about the fake shakes. The majority of the students experienced the vibrations, but, as *Slate* magazine explains, the study found it happened more often to extroverts and neurotics:

> Extroverts, the theory goes, check their phones a lot because keeping in touch with friends is a big part of their lives. Neurotics, meanwhile, worry a lot about the status of their relationships—so while they may not get as many text messages, they care a lot about what they say.

In any event, most researchers think that the fake vibrations are harmless (albeit annoying)—although there has been very little research into that.

BONUS FACT

The 1969 *Apollo 11* moon landing is a favorite topic of conspiracy theorists who assert that the landing was faked and instead filmed on a sound stage. In September 2002, one such conspiracy theorist physically accosted the second man on the moon, Buzz Aldrin (whose mother's maiden name was Moon!), demanding he swear upon a Bible (that the conspiracy theorist brought with him) that the landing was faked. Instead, Aldrin punched the guy. Authorities declined to press charges against Aldrin.

UN-SILENT PICTURES
CLICKING FOR SAFETY

Take out your cell phone and take a picture. If the sound is on, you may hear a shutter sound—something (if you're old enough) reminiscent of the nondigital cameras of yesteryear. That sound is artificial, and likely included to bring the full camera-like experience to the digital world. With most phones, if you want to turn off the sound, you can. Apple's iPhone 3G, for example, has no shutter sound if you put your phone in silent mode.

Except in Japan.

As the Apple-aficionado site Cult of Mac reported, the digital revolution led to a perverse de-evolution of proper public conduct among some Japanese. The new trend? "Upskirt" and "downblouse" photos of women, taken without their permission and often without their knowledge. To make this violation worse, the increasing popularity of social media means that a victim's image could spread widely, potentially with enough context to identify the person depicted. The problem got so out of hand that most subway stations now have signs warning to "Watch out for upskirting."

To help prevent this, the Japanese version of the iPhone 3G—and many subsequent models—kept the shutter sound even if a user set the phone to silent. While this wouldn't stop the most brazen upskirt photogs, the hope was pretty clear. At the very least, it would draw attention to what they were doing.

So far, this requirement isn't widespread outside Japan. However, in 2009, U.S. Congressman Peter King wanted to do the same thing in the United States, introducing a bill called the Camera Phone Predator Alert Act, which, if enacted, would "require mobile phones containing digital cameras to make a sound when a photograph is taken." The bill did not receive support from any other legislators and never became law.

But even if the bill were to have become law, it wouldn't have mattered much, if Japan is any indicator. Those intent on taking such photos surreptitiously have found workarounds. For phones running Google's Android operating system, there are apps that, according to the *Daily Mail,* override the system settings and mute the shutter sound. There's an even easier work-around—for most phones, using a headset pushes all noise to the ear buds, effectively muzzling the sound.

BONUS FACT

In August 2010, Boston police set up a sting operation to catch a man who was reported to be taking upskirt photos in the city's subway system. The case made its way to the highest court in Massachusetts, which, on March 5, 2014, ruled that the man wasn't guilty of anything—the law only pertains to photographs taken of subjects who are at least "partially nude." The court ruled that "a female passenger [. . .] who is wearing a skirt, dress, or the like covering these parts of her body is not a person who is 'partially nude,' no matter what is or is not underneath the skirt by way of underwear or other clothing." If you think that's ridiculous, you're not alone—the Massachusetts government passed a revised version of the law two days later.

CHIKANNERY
THE UNDERGROUND WOMEN-ONLY CLUB

The Japanese term *chikan* means "street groping," and the fact that there's a specific term for such an act speaks volumes about the extent of the problem. This is especially true when it comes to the subway. According to the *Guardian*, locals dubbed Osaka's railway the "Pervert Express," while a 2001 survey of Tokyo high schoolers found that 70 percent of female students had been victims of at least one such assault on the trains in their area. Another survey, one conducted by the Tokyo police in conjunction with the East Japan Railway Company, found that two-thirds of women between the ages of twenty and forty had been groped at least once.

Over the past decade or two, officials have tried to change this, with stricter sentencing for those convicted of the crime and awareness campaigns to help bring the issue to light, but by and large, these have not been very successful. While awareness and enforcement efforts have led to an increased number of victims filing reports, many victims are embarrassed to come forward. The problem is still widely believed to be rampant if not entirely out of control.

One of the newer solutions? Segregated trains.

Specifically, many Japanese transit providers have taken to providing women-only train cars. These cars were first introduced in 2000, when a private railway that provides service from Tokyo to the suburbs tested the concept during late-night runs. Over the five or so years subsequent, most other railways adopted a similar option, finding the offering popular (which should surprise no one). Even a large percentage of men approve of the addition of these cars. As ABC News pointed out, crowded trains lead to potentially false accusations of *chikan* (or of victims wrongly accusing an innocent man of committing his neighbor's indiscretion), and at a fine of around $500 and up to seven years in prison, that's something best avoided.

Interestingly, there's no fine or threat of incarceration if a man gets on a women-only car. Doing so isn't illegal, according to *Japan Today*. The rule, to the extent that it truly is one, is enforced by shaming. In an odd sense, the same thing that keeps women from reporting *chikan*—embarrassment—keeps men from violating the commuting space of Japanese straphangers. The term "women only" is somewhat inaccurate as well, as young children, the disabled, and some other males are customarily allowed in the cars.

Regardless, the innovation has proven successful and has found a home in other transit systems throughout the world. India, Brazil, Mexico, and a handful of other places have female-only transit options, aiming to stem a similar problem to the one encapsulated by the term *chikan*.

BONUS FACT

In 2001, Dubai opened up a women-only bank. As the BBC reported, the purpose was to give women in the highly conservative country a way to manage their finances without having to explain their transactions to the men in their lives. Specifically, the BBC noted that "in some cases," the goal of the bank was to provide the customers some "secrecy from their husbands." It didn't work well, and most people forgot about it, as evidenced by the fact that seven years later, another bank with special amenities catering to women only opened in Dubai—and the *L.A. Times* called it "the first of its kind." (Oops!)

GIVING NO CREDIT
THE PLASTIC PIECE OF DISCRIMINATION IN YOUR WALLET (IN THE 1970s)

Roughly 75 percent of American adults have a credit card in their name, and especially now with the ubiquity of e-commerce, credit-card use is commonplace. Competition among credit companies to sign up new cardholders is fierce, and it's not difficult to get offered a line of credit. More than 40 percent of U.S. households carry some level of credit-card debt, and the average indebted household owes more than $15,000 on those cards. It seems as if getting a credit card is not only easy but inevitable, especially when the companies come offering some sort of incentive to sign up—air miles, cash back, rewards points, and the like.

However, until 1974, if you were a woman who wanted a credit card, it wasn't so easy. You usually needed a job or some other regular source of income. You needed some level of savings and a much better credit history than your male counterparts. One other thing:

You needed to get married first—and stay that way.

For much of human history, men were considered the breadwinners and women the homemakers to a degree bordering on the absolute. Only in rare cases did women work, and when they did, it was only in a narrow set of jobs—teachers and nurses, for example. Society often concluded that women weren't up to tasks such as balancing a checkbook or paying bills; that was left to the man, as keeper of the household's finances. In general, the banking industry held strongly to these gender norms, only providing services to men. In the early 1970s, those services included lines of credit and the plastic cards that went with them.

For unmarried women, this was especially problematic. The Equal Pay Act of 1963 and Title VII of the Civil Rights Act of 1964 barred gender-based discrimination in matters of employment, helping usher in a society where women were able to earn a living for themselves. Younger, single women (of childbearing age) could now find work as employers couldn't reject female applicants on the grounds that they'd get married and leave their jobs to have kids. Banks, however, were not barred from holding and acting on such beliefs. Many banks refused to issue credit cards to these women, believing they'd stop working once pregnant, be unable to pay off their debt, and their husbands-to-be, seeing this problem and not wanting to assume their future wives' credit problems, would find ways around assuming that debt.

For divorced women, the problem was even more ludicrous: Many banking institutions assumed that if a woman couldn't manage a marriage, she certainly couldn't manage a credit card—so no credit for them, either. If they were still married, though? In that case, credit was available—but only with their husband's permission and signature. Credit-card companies would typically only allow a woman to count her own income on the application, not the household's, and any earnings she had came with the concerns addressed previously. In practice, this meant that women of the early 1970s typically couldn't have their own credit cards.

What changed? The law. In 1974, the federal government passed the Equal Credit Opportunity Act, which prohibited discrimination on the basis of gender when making credit decisions and further allowed applicants to include household income (i.e., a wife could include her husband's) in the application process.

BONUS FACT

As noted earlier, there have been a few occupations that have been historically filled by women. Among that (short) list is the now-antiquated telephone switchboard operator. The first telephone switchboard operators were male—typically boys in their late teens and early twenties—but in 1878, the Boston Telephone Dispatch company grew tired of their employees' lack of patience, inattentiveness, and their proclivity to curse and play pranks on customers whose calls they were supposed to be directing. On September 1 of that year, the company hired a woman named Emma Nutt as the world's first female telephone switchboard operator. According to Wikipedia, "The customer response to her soothing, cultured voice and patience was overwhelmingly positive." That sparked off a trend, and for decades thereafter, telephone operators were predominantly female.

REVERSING THE CHARGES
HOW ONE MAN FOUGHT BACK AGAINST HIS CREDIT-CARD COMPANY

Twenty thousand words. That's roughly the equivalent of a thirty- to forty-page high school term paper. But in this case, the documents in question weren't written by a tenth grader comparing and contrasting *1984* and *Brave New World.* They were written by a team of attorneys, and those 20,000 or so words probably need another team of attorneys if you want to comprehend the documents' meaning. Yet we consumers sign these contracts anyway. They're credit-card agreements.

That word count comes courtesy of the *Wall Street Journal,* which further notes that as recently as 1980, the typical credit-card agreement ran a mere 400 words—a page and a half or so. For most of us, though, it hardly matters whether the agreement is two pages or two hundred; we're going to sign it anyway and we're not going to read it beforehand. A Russian man named Dmitry Argarkov wondered if the same was true for the credit-card companies themselves—did they read the fine-print? To test, he added some of his own.

Tinkoff Credit Systems, "Russia's leading provider of online financial services," according to the company's website (as of the summer of 2013), offers three types of credit cards, and a quick perusal of their benefits suggests nothing out of the ordinary. You can earn points, air miles, etc., simply by using your card (and paying your bills, of course), just like one would expect in the United States and points elsewhere. According to the *Telegraph*, Argarkov was offered a credit card by Tinkoff, but Argarkov wasn't interested in their offer—the interest rates were too high. While most people would simply toss the offer letter in the trash, Argarkov got creative. He made a counter-offer.

The terms were, to say the least, very favorable to Mr. Argarkov. His card, if the contract he re-drafted were enforceable, came with a zero-percent interest rate, no credit limit, and of course, no fees. He still had to pay his balance, though, but this seemed like a bad deal for the credit-card company. Tinkoff could try and enforce their original offer, but Argarkov put in a penalty of 3 million rubles (about $90,000) for each such violation of his terms. If Tinkoff wanted to cancel the card outright, they could—but they'd have to pay a 6 million ruble ($180,000) cancellation fee. Tinkoff did neither—instead, they signed Argarkov's revised term sheet.

Then, Argarkov failed to pay his balance. Why not? With no fees and the zero-percent interest rate, there was no pressing need to do so. Of course, Tinkoff didn't realize this, as no one had read through his revisions. So Tinkoff canceled the card, citing a long-overdue balance, and sued their former cardholder for 45,000 rubles—19,000 from the charges themselves, and another 26,000 in fines and interest. Argarkov's defense cited his changes to the document, and the judge agreed that he only owed the 19,000 rubles ($575, give or take).

As for the penalties? Argarkov countersued, seeking 24 million rubles ($360,000) in damages. That suit was to hit the Russian courts in September 2013. Tinkoff thought that it would ultimately prevail; its CEO and founder, Oleg Tinkoff, tweeted that the company's lawyers were confident that Argarkov wouldn't get the money. Rather, Tinkoff asserted, Argarkov would receive jail time for fraud.

Neither happened; the case never saw the inside of a courtroom. The two sides settled, agreeing to call it even.

BONUS FACT

If you're a purchaser of, say, adult-only content online and buy such content using a credit card, make sure that the name you use is male. According to a 2011 article in the *Wall Street Journal*, the major billing company used by that audience "flags female names as potential fraud, since so many of these charges result in an angry wife or mother demanding a refund for the misuse of her card." (No word on whether the popularity of *Fifty Shades of Grey* changed that.)

MEAL TICKET
HOW MOSCOW'S HOMELESS DOGS LEARNED TO WORK THE SYSTEM FOR FREE MEALS

It's hard to find an urban area that does not have a significant homeless population. Be it New York, San Francisco, Tokyo, or Madrid, you're likely to encounter someone for whom life has dealt a bad hand. Some homeless have taken creative measures to adapt, finding ways to persevere in the concrete and asphalt wilderness around them. In one city, this will to survive is not solely in the domain of the human homeless.

Meet the homeless, subway-riding dogs of Moscow.

There are about 35,000 homeless dogs in Russia's capital, roaming the streets and alleys looking for a meal. Most of them are feral and eschew contact with people. However, about 500 or so have done what many homeless people have done and become semi-permanent denizens of the subways—in this case, the Moscow Metro. The advantages are more than just a roof and associated shelter from the weather. The dogs can cozy up to riders in hopes of getting food tossed their way, or, if opportunity knocks, scare an unsuspecting train-goer into dropping his or her snack. Either way, this newfound meal is critical to the hungry subway-living dog.

For about two dozen or so dogs, though, the bark-and-eat gambit is merely a start. These advanced dogs have taken the subway game to the next level: They have become commuters. Areas with office buildings are crowded during the day but sparsely populated during the early mornings and late evenings; meanwhile, the opposite pattern is found in residential neighborhoods. Therefore, it behooves panhandlers, canine and human alike, to be near the offices at lunch time and near people's homes at night. So, some Metro pups do exactly that—as reported by both ABC News and the *Sun* newspaper, the dogs have figured out how to navigate the train network to optimize their locations throughout the day.

And they do so in style. The dogs have figured out which trains offer more room, so they can curl up on a bench for an in-transit snooze.

BONUS FACT

In 1980, the *New York Times* reported that the typical price of a single slice of pizza had matched, "with uncanny precision," the price of a single ride on New York's subway system since the 1960s. The *Times* revisited the strange correlation in 2002 and determined that it was still true.

THE SUBMARINE SUBWAY
WHAT SUBWAY TRAINS TURN INTO WHEN THEY'RE NO LONGER USED

The Metropolitan Transit Authority (MTA) is responsible for the mass transit needs of the greater New York City area. As part of its services, the MTA operates more than 6,000 train cars over 800 miles of track. Those 6,500-plus vehicles have a lifespan of thirty to forty years before they wear out and are no longer viable for use.

Then they go to sleep with the fishes.

Really.

For decades, the MTA has been running a program to turn disused subway cars into artificial reefs, situated off the Mid-Atlantic coast of the United States. The MTA pays to remove the doors, wheels, and windows from each train car, as well as clean off any hazardous materials (such as some petroleum-based lubricants), which federal law prohibits from being dumped into the ocean. Then the cars—more than 1,500 of them—are shipped off to New Jersey, Delaware, Maryland, South Carolina, and Georgia. Once there, the cars are loaded onto barges equipped with specialized cranes and dumped into the ocean just a few miles off shore.

In doing so, the MTA and its partners have not only managed to find an environmentally sound way of disposing of these hulking transports but also revitalized the Atlantic fishing industry. Before the subway cars landed in the Atlantic, the relatively barren waterways weren't a good place for fish to hang out, as natural predators could easily hunt them down in the open water. That changed when the trains arrived. As one Delaware official told Reuters, "a 600-car reef in that state's waters had increased the local fish population by 400 times, and boosted the number of angling trips to 13,000 a year from 300 before the reef was created." As an added benefit, crab, mussels, and shrimp also have begun to colonize on many of the reefs.

Many of those concerned about the environment and the ecology of the oceans are fans of these artificial reefs. While there have been some problems, most notably in New Jersey where some cars deteriorated faster than expected, these projects are generally seen as a resounding success. In 2007, according to a report by transit blog Second Avenue Sagas, train cars that had been submerged for nearly a decade and a half were still 67 percent intact.

In part because of these successes, other man-made items have been tossed to the bottom of the sea in hopes of creating a similar home for fish and their friends. Perhaps the most notable example: in May 2006, the U.S. Navy intentionally sank the long-decommissioned USS *Oriskany*, a 900-foot-long aircraft carrier. It now sits on the floor of the Gulf of Mexico off the coast of Pensacola. Not only is it a great place for marine life, but if you're a recreational diver, it's close enough to shore that you can go pay it a visit.

BONUS FACT

In a previous bonus fact we discussed the odd correlation between the price of a pizza slice in New York City and the price of a Big Apple subway ride. However, the fate of a pizza box and a subway car couldn't be more different. While subway cars are recycled, as noted previously, pizza boxes often can't be. According to the city's sanitation department, cardboard (and for that matter, paper) that is contaminated with food should go into the trash, as "the food particles, greases, and oils leave residues that are contaminants and aren't recyclable."

ONE'S TRASH, ANOTHER'S TREASURE

THE UNLIKELY BLACK MARKET THAT STARTS IN YOUR RECYCLE BIN

There's an old saying: "One man's trash is another man's treasure," the origin of which has been lost to time. The saying is a commentary on how there is no accounting for taste—what one person may think is worthless may be cherished by another. In the case of one type of refuse, the literal meaning of the phrase rings true—to the point of fueling organized crime in parts of the United States.

That product? Old cardboard boxes. While some people are trying to throw them out, others are stealing them before the waste haulers come by.

Cardboard boxes are recyclable. As recyclables go, they make for some of the best garbage out there. They are easy to transport because they can be baled up and thrown in the back of a truck, allowing tons of cardboard to be carted for miles without much labor or fuel costs. The recycling process itself is centered on something called a hydropulper, a moving bath of warm water that mixes the bales until the cardboard turns into an oatmeal-like paper pulp. That pulp can be turned back into boxes or other products made of corrugated fiberboard.

Because cardboard boxes have a second life, they have value even after they are emptied of their contents and sent off with the waste hauler. While municipalities and companies alike will pay such service providers to take their garbage and recyclables away, the haulers also make money by selling the bales of cardboard to recyclers. However, others are aware of cardboard's value—approximately $100 a ton—and grab it before the haulers can. Because the waste management companies have contractually agreed to take the trash (at a price lower than they would if the recyclable cardboard were not present), taking cardboard is often considered theft.

One notable such crime spree involved three New Jersey men who, over the course of four months, made off with over 900 tons of cardboard, as reported by *Metro* in Philadelphia. While most cardboard runners simply steal the boxes lying on the side of the road (which is typical in larger cities) or from behind large stores like Walmart or Target, the New Jersey trio was more creative. They created a sham corporation called "Metro Paper, Inc." and rented trucks. Then, they monitored the pickup schedules at large stores that went through a high volume of boxes. Once they had the schedule down, the men made sure they arrived before the legitimate haulers, picking up the boxes and moving on to their next target.

Seem like a waste of time—or a crime not worth the risk? According to Waste Recycling News, the group sold their treasure trove of used cardboard boxes for just north of $100,000.

BONUS FACT

What does society do with all those recycled boxes? Usually they're turned into more boxes, as noted previously. However, Israeli inventor Izhar Gafni, a bicycling enthusiast, decided to take his hobby and turn it into a challenge. As reported by Fast Company, Gafni built a fully functional bike out of recycled cardboard boxes. The water-resistant bicycle used only $9 in materials.

IN THE LIME OF FIRE
WHEN DRUG CARTELS GARNISH GARNISHES

If you're in the United States and there's a lime nearby, it's almost certain that the little green citrus in question came from Mexico. The United States imports nearly all of its limes—95 percent—from its neighbor to the south, and typically, supplies are stable and therefore, so are prices. In recent years, limes sold for about $20 for a thirty-eight-pound case (wholesale), according to a *PBS News-hour* report. However, in the early part of 2014, the prices spiked five-fold and remained there for a few months. In mid-May, prices restabilized, and the prices of limes fell back to their traditional levels.

In most cases, the lime-producing farmers would be cheering on the era of expensive limes and bemoaning the subsequent price crash. In this case, though, the opposite was true. The higher prices went, the more scared farmers became for their lives and livelihoods. When the price returned to normal, it was because something great had happened.

It meant the drug lords had gone away.

The lime wars started innocently enough. Toward the end of 2013, heavy rains in some parts of Mexico's lime-producing regions damaged crops while bacteria invaded another region. (A person with an affinity for puns may point out that parts of Mexico had to deal with a particularly bad epidemic of lime disease.) Supply fell, demand stayed roughly the same, and the basic rules of economics kicked in, leading to a small but noticeable uptick in the price of limes. If you were one of the affected farmers, hopefully you had diversified your crops or had banked some money in case of bad times. On the other hand, if you had limes to sell, it was a good day, as you made a little more profit than usual.

If you were a drug cartel, you suddenly had access to a product you could import into the United States without risking incarceration or worse.

The cartel in question is the Templarios—the Knights Templar, in English—a criminal organization active in the Mexican state of Michoacán. The Templarios aren't just drug smugglers—they're more akin to the Mafia than anything else, with a history of kidnapping, counterfeiting, money laundering, arms trafficking, and murder. In many areas of Michoacán, there's a good chance that any businessman you meet is paying protection money to the Templarios. For his sake, he probably should be.

Despite this criminal activity, Michoacán has experienced an agricultural boom over the past few years, and limes are one of the largest growth areas. Going into 2014, six contiguous towns in Michoacán are, collectively, responsible for about 20 percent of the limes produced nationwide. That many limes in such a small, easily managed area was too good for the Templarios to resist. According to the *Washington Post*, the drug-fueled cartel used its muscle to slow the production of limes while taking ownership of the citrus supply chain. The Templarios bought up lime farms, often extorting the previous owners to sell for cheap or face threat of violence, then drastically reduced output. Many other lime farms were *de facto* operated by the Templarios, and they cut production as well. For those farmers who were somehow outside the control of the Knights Templar, they had few places that would take their fruit—food packagers were understandably wary, given the possible (if not probable) repercussions.

Ultimately, many in Michoacán started to join militias and took up arms against the Templarios. Mexico's federal government also sent in police, and the lime cartel began to crumble. NPR reported that "several top leaders [of the Templarios were] killed or arrested"and the limes began to flow freely once again.

BONUS FACT

According to a 2002 article in the *Washington Post*, escaping from jail isn't illegal in Mexico. Yes, if you're caught, you still have to go back and serve out your jail term—but authorities don't tack on any additional time because of your attempt to gain some freedom a bit early. Juventino Victor Castro y Castro, then one of Mexico's Supreme Court justices, explained to the press that "the basic desire for freedom is implicit inside every man, so trying to escape cannot be considered a crime."

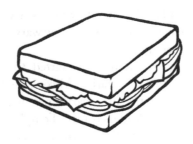

SANDWICH LAW
LEGALLY SPEAKING, WHAT MAKES SOMETHING A SANDWICH?

There are many Mexican restaurant chains in the United States, most notably Chipotle, Qdoba, Taco del Mar, and Moe's Southwest Grill. Go into any and order a burrito and you'll get what's known as a "San Francisco" or "Mission-style" burrito. These burritos differ from their Mexican progenitors in size—they're just plain bigger—and by the number of items stuffed inside them—there's a lot more. It's a meal by any measure.

But is it a sandwich?

To most, such a question wouldn't matter. When the San Francisco burrito was created by a Mission-district grocer named Febronio Ontiveros in the early 1960s, he probably didn't care about the semantics. All Ontiveros cared about were the local firefighters who were hungry and wanted sandwiches—and the fact that he was out of bread other than some six-inch tortillas. So he threw meat, rice, and bunch of other items in it, rolled it up, and sold it for a dollar. The product—and price—has gotten larger since, but the item has maintained its defining traits. Whether the firefighters (or for that matter, Ontiveros) thought of it as a sandwich or a replacement product is anyone's guess. However, in 2006, a judge in Massachusetts had to make that guess.

Panera Bread operated a franchise at the White City Shopping Center in the Massachusetts town of Shrewsbury. In its lease, Panera had a clause preventing the shopping mall's operators from renting out space to another sandwich shop. White City offered to lease a spot to Qdoba, and Panera invoked this clause to prevent it. Qdoba and White City argued that Qdoba wasn't selling sandwiches; Panera countered by noting that Qdoba offered burritos, and argued that burritos are sandwiches.

The matter went to judge Jeffrey Locke who, according to the Associated Press, turned to Webster's Dictionary and a few expert witnesses. He concluded that a burrito was not, in fact, a sandwich: "A sandwich is not commonly understood to include burritos, tacos, and quesadillas, which are typically made with a single tortilla and stuffed with a choice filling of meat, rice, and beans." With that Qdoba was able to move into the White City mall.

But in the end, Panera got the last laugh. As of this writing, the Qdoba at White City is no longer in business, but the Panera Bread is.

BONUS FACT

There's some argument to be made that the sandwich-ish thing called a wrap is a spinoff of the San Francisco burrito, as it may have been invented in the mid-1990s by a Mission-area restaurant called World Wrapps. (There's a competing story, which is probably hogwash, that former Major League Baseball manager Bobby Valentine invented the wrap in 1980 at his Stamford, Connecticut, restaurant.) So is a wrap a sandwich? There's no consensus. As reported by the *Harvard Crimson*, the *Oxford Encyclopedia of Food and Drink in America* asserts that they are sandwiches. Nonetheless, the wrap's burrito-kin history would suggest otherwise—as would the helpfully named website *www.IsAWrapASandwich.com*. (If you go there, you'll see that the website has one word on it: "No.")

COURTING TOMATOES
ARE TOMATOES FRUITS OR VEGETABLES? YES!

Tomatoes are a fruit. No, they're a vegetable. No wait—they're a fruit.

The truth: they're both. The two groups are not mutually exclusive. But if you're the American legal system, well, only one of the two definitions matters.

Fruits, botanically speaking, are the seed-containing ovaries of a flowering plant—and yes, this definition includes the tomato, as well as cucumbers, which are also often referred to as a vegetable.

This is because the term "vegetable" lacks scientific meaning and instead is defined loosely by the culture of food. When and how a specific food is served determines how the food is categorized. For example, plants that are most commonly used in soups, salads, or as side dishes to a main course are typically considered vegetables. This includes tomatoes and cucumbers, as well as sweet corn (a grain whose kernels are the fruit) and mushrooms (which is a fungus, not a plant). So while the term "vegetable" generally refers to the edible parts of plants other than the fruit or seeds, that distinction is imprecise and incomplete.

Tomatoes, therefore, are both fruits *and* veggies, and if you ask linguistic experts (and many dictionaries), you'll find them generally in agreement over the matter.

Much ado about nothing? Perhaps, but the U.S. Supreme Court found the issue important enough to address. In 1883, the U.S. government passed a tariff act, requiring that importers of vegetables pay a tax—a tax that did not apply to the importation of fruits. Ten years later, in *Nix v. Hedden*, a group of tomato importers filed suit against the government. The importers hoped to recover taxes already paid by arguing that botanically, tomatoes were a fruit and therefore not subject to the tariff. In a unanimous decision, the Court held in favor of the government. Noting that tomatoes were used typically with main courses and not as desserts, the Court concluded that tomatoes were subject to the import tax.

At the state level, three states—Arkansas, Ohio, and Tennessee—call the tomato the state fruit. (In Arkansas, it is actually the official fruit/vegetable.) However, this is not unanimous: In 2005, New Jersey relied on the reasoning in *Nix* when it considered making the tomato its official vegetable of the state.

BONUS FACT

In 2000, police in Blacksburg, Virginia, kept receiving 911 calls from the home of local residents Daniel and Linda Hurst—but when the emergency operator spoke, no one on the Hursts' end spoke. After determining that the Hursts were not home, the police decided to raid the home, guns drawn, to search for potential hostages or malfeasants. They found neither. Instead, they found an overripe tomato, dripping its juice onto an answering machine. This caused the answering machine to short circuit and, for some reason, repeatedly dial 911. Apparently, tomatoes are fruits, vegetables, and, in the right context, prank callers.

IN LINE FOR JUSTICE
THE COST OF GOING TO THE SUPREME COURT

The Supreme Court of the United States hears arguments from October through April. Photography and videography are prohibited, and therefore there are few opportunities to watch the proceedings in action. Unless you're working for the Court, are an attorney arguing the case, or one of the lucky few reporters to sit in the front rows of the visitors' gallery, you may be out of luck. There are about fifty or so seats open to the public, and the good news is that they're free, on a first-come, first-served basis. The bad news is that the line is usually at least a few hours long, so unless you're willing to get there early, you are unlikely to find yourself getting one of those few dozen seats.

Or you can buy one on the black market.

The problem is a simple, Econ 101 one—there's a scarce supply of seats and a lot more demand. Waiting in line, beyond being terribly boring, isn't a very good use of most people's time, including many of the people who truly want to be inside the courthouse when the nine Justices listen to arguments and pepper the attorneys with questions. This is America, though—so someone has turned the wait into cash. In some cases, a lot of cash.

For decades, people in the Beltway have volunteered to sit in line for you, for a fee. In 2005, according to a report by the *Washington Post*, a man named Kevin Rollins earned $350 for waiting in line on behalf of a law firm. The firm wanted one of its clients, whom it was representing in front of the Court, to be able to listen to the arguments, but the length of the line proved prohibitive. Rollins spent fourteen hours waiting on behalf of the law firm and its client for an hourly rate of $25.

In years since, line standing has become a boom industry in the Beltway. At least two different businesses in the Beltway have entered the market, playing the matchmaker role—for a cut, they'll find a line-stander for you, and for very long assignments, they'll find relief placeholders as needed. Prices have shot up to at least $50 an hour, and lines have gotten longer, sometimes requiring line sitters to hang out for two or three days. According to one report, one keep-my-place-in-line assignment for a highly visible case cost the purchaser $6,000. Note that observers do not have an opportunity to influence the case; they are, as the name suggests, merely there to watch the goings-on.

The businesses providing these services also tend to provide similar services for those who wish to attend congressional hearings, much to the chagrin of at least one senator. In 2007, Senator Claire McCaskill from Missouri proposed legislation to ban the practice, but as of this writing, any such efforts have been to no avail.

BONUS FACT

Next time you're waiting in line, say, to check out at a store, try to guess how long your wait was. You're probably overestimating significantly. According to retail researcher and environmental psychologist Paco Underhill, we can only wait in line for about ninety seconds before we lose our perception of time. After that, Underhill observes, we begin to think that significantly more time has passed than actually has—a three-minute wait, for example, feels more like five.

CAN'T HARDLY WAIT
WHEN SOON ISN'T SOON ENOUGH

Worst. Thing. Ever.

You've probably seen or heard someone say that, usually in a half-facetious, half-hyperbolic sense. (Or because you've watched the *Simpsons* and know who the Comic Book Guy, originator of the line, is.) When (real) people use that phrase, isolated as three individual pseudo-sentences for effect, they're not talking about actual terrible things like famine, the plague, or the Nazis. They're talking about the minor inconveniences that bother us in an amount disproportional to the actual harm we suffer. A quick search of Twitter elicits things like "not having somewhere to park my car," "chapped lips," and "having short hair on rainy days" as examples of things that were considered the "worst thing ever" by the Tweeter in question.

Here's another one: waiting.

Waiting is a particularly fiendish terror, which evokes the hyperbole just mentioned. People bemoan having to visit the Department of Motor Vehicles, grumble when YouTube videos take more than a half-second to load, and, as some airport executives in Houston learned, complain when it takes too long for their bags to come. We'd rather do anything other than, well, do nothing.

Unfortunately, we can't eliminate waiting altogether, and in some cases, even a relatively short wait may be too long. That's what the Houston airport execs learned when they answered passengers' complaints directly. Customers were waiting for a long while, perhaps as long as a half hour, for their bags to arrive. The airport beefed up staff and cut the wait time down to eight minutes—as the *New York Times* noted, that's "well within industry benchmarks." Yet the complaints just kept coming. That's kind of ridiculous—it's only eight minutes!—but regardless, customers still weren't happy. To make matters worse, there wasn't much the airport team could do to get the bags back to the flyers in less time. Eight minutes from disembark until the bags hit the carousel was as good as it was going to get.

But saying "deal with it!" is bad customer service, and really, no one wants to hear complaints from customers. So, as the *Times* explained, the powers that be at the Houston airport decided to just trick the passengers into thinking they weren't waiting. They observed that customers at other airports weren't complaining about baggage claims that weren't all that close to the arrival gates, yet the Houston airport only required passengers to walk for about a minute to get their stuff. On the other hand, Houston's customers were very upset about having to stand around for seven of the eight minutes. It wasn't the eight-minute delay, itself, that was the problem—it was that people hated the idea that they were wasting time, doing nothing.

The solution? The airport moved the arrival gates and the baggage claim carousels farther apart. Much farther. The formerly one-minute walk to get one's bag was now six minutes, and the idle wait only about two. The travelers were occupied for longer and therefore less bored, and the complaints disappeared.

BONUS FACT

The International Air Transit Association assigns three-letter airport codes to each airport, typically comprised of the first three letters of the city the airport is located in. There are many exceptions, though, and in those cases, a close-ish approximation of the airport's or city's name is used instead. New York City, for example, has both LaGuardia and Kennedy, which are LGA and JFK, as they can't start with N—the navy has that reserved. But what about LAX in Los Angeles? The X doesn't stand for anything—it's just a placeholder. "LA," the airport's original code, is unambiguous, but when the three-character codes became standard, the airport needed to expand its code. It adopted a meaningless X at the end.

DINNER AND A BACKUP PLAN
WHY PILOTS AND COPILOTS CAN'T SHARE A MEAL

Redundancy and efficiency don't go well together. We wear belts *or* suspenders, not *and*, because having both would be unnecessary and the extra cost or discomfort isn't worth it. Sometimes, though, having a backup plan is a good idea, especially when the risk of failure is incredibly high. If you are operating a commercial airline, for example, it makes a lot of sense to have a pilot and a copilot, because if something happens to the pilot, you really need someone who can still fly the plane. Even if it ends up costing a little more.

Copilots are trained to do everything a pilot does, in case of emergency. However, there's one thing, for most airlines at least, that the copilot can't do. He or she cannot have the same meal as the pilot.

The copilot's job isn't simply to be the backup—he or she assists in takeoffs, landings, and in a variety of in-flight duties, making sure that everything is being done properly and that the safety and best-practices checklists are followed. While most modern planes can be piloted by one person if need be, that's not a great idea, as people make mistakes (and in this case, mistakes can have massive consequences). In November 2012, for example, the copilot of a

Lufthansa flight from Newark, New Jersey, to Frankfurt, Germany, became ill, and an off-duty pilot for another airline, who happened to be a passenger, helped land the plane. (The plane diverted to Dublin, Ireland, due to the copilot's illness.) While the passenger's skills lessened the potential problem, it isn't fair to say he prevented a disaster, though; the flight crew could have assisted the pilot sufficiently to land the plane safely—most likely.

It's rare, however, that both the pilot and copilot will become incapacitated, save for something truly nefarious such as a hijacking. One exception? Food poisoning. As recounted by a *New York Times* article from March 1984, there have been numerous times when flights were put at risk by contaminated food. In 1982, for example, a flight from Boston to Lisbon had to return to Massachusetts after both the pilot and copilot (and six others) fell ill from eating bad tapioca pudding. In 1975, roughly a third of a 364-person flight going from Tokyo to Paris became ill after eating eggs containing staphylococcal bacteria. The only reason the pilot and copilot didn't get sick? Their internal clocks were on a different schedule, and instead of eating breakfast, they dined on steak—dinner. The *Times* article advocated for rules that prevented pilot and copilot from sharing meals, something not regulated at the time.

As the BBC reported in 2009, that has mostly changed. That year, the pilot on a Continental flight from Brussels to Newark died in mid-flight; however, the flight ended safely. As the BBC noted, "The main reason for having two pilots is that something like this occasionally happens—though it's less common for a pilot to die than to be incapacitated by something like food poisoning." Because of that concern, today's airlines, by and large, require that the copilot not eat the same meals as the pilot.

Who gets first choice? That's left unreported, but it would be surprising if the head pilot doesn't get that privilege.

BONUS FACT

Making good-tasting airline food is very difficult, perhaps for a surprising reason. According to Alaska Airlines' corporate chef Clifton Lyles (via NPR), at an airplane's cruising altitude, our taste buds are about 25 percent less effective than normal. From the article: "As the cabin is pressurized and the humidity inside the plane falls, some of your taste buds go numb, and your sense of smell is diminished, too. Things that tasted great on the ground are now bland and boring."

BEN'S BIG DECISION
THE RIGHT MAN IN THE RIGHT PLACE AT THE WORST TIME

On September 11, 2001, terrorists hijacked four American commercial jets with the intention of crashing them into large, visible buildings in Washington, DC, and New York City. As we all know, the terrorists were successful in three of the four cases; the fourth plane's assault on the United States Capitol—the presumed target—was thwarted by the heroic passengers on board. While we now believe that no other planes were targeted, each of the other 4,000-plus flights scheduled to be in American air space at the time were at risk. But Ben Sliney, the Federal Aviation Commission's National Operations Manager on duty that morning, prevented future harm.

How? He made an unprecedented decision, grounding every single commercial airplane in the country.

That, of course, is not news—in fact, it's common knowledge. While hindsight teaches us that the call was correct, at the time it was an aggressive decision. Thankfully, it was the type of decision that Sliney was well equipped to make. He had twenty-five years of experience in air traffic control and/or as part of FAA management, including a leadership position at New York TRACON, which has responsibility over the air traffic for New York City's three major airports and a few smaller regional airports nearby. His position as National Operations Manager gave him immediate access to information as it became available. But the decision to ground the planes—that was Sliney's to consider, and ultimately, to make.

In all, Ben Sliney's initiative makes for an incredible story. When Universal Pictures decided to turn the heroism of the passengers of United Flight 93 into a movie, they did not overlook Ben Sliney's role—they even asked him to play himself in the movie.

As incredible as his story is, one particular fact makes it jaw dropping: On September 10, 2001, Ben Sliney was not yet a National Operations Manager for the FAA. September 11, 2001, was Sliney's first day on the job.

BONUS FACT

During the three-day ban on commercial flights after the September 11 attacks, very few planes were in the sky—by and large, air traffic was limited to military flights. (One exception? A San Diego to Miami flight, authorized to take flight in order to deliver antivenin to a snake-bite victim.) Because of the lack of planes, there was also a lack of contrails, those white, cloud-like tracks planes leave in the sky. The lack of contrails corresponded to a measurable, significant increase in temperature, leading some to believe that contrails help depress global warming—a theory echoed by World War II data as well.

SUPER-SECRET SUCTION
THE CIA'S TOP SECRET ANTI-TERRORISM VACUUM CLEANER SCHEMATICS THAT MAY OR MAY NOT EXIST

Vacuum cleaners are pretty great tools. Modern ones can clean kitchen floors, get dust and grime in hard-to-reach places, and of course, clean your carpet. They may even help U.S. government officials thwart a future terrorist attack.

But we don't know, because that's classified.

You've probably heard of Khalid Sheikh Mohammed. The U.S. government, in the official commission report on the September 11, 2001 attacks, deemed Mohammed the "principle architect" of the attacks and has kept him under lock and key since his capture in 2003, most recently in the Guantanamo Bay Naval Prison. Under what officials call "enhanced interrogation techniques," Mohammed has admitted to masterminding not only the events of 9/11 but also the 1993 World Trade Center bombing, the attempted "shoe-bombing" in December of 2001, and various other terrorist attacks.

These "enhanced interrogation techniques" are controversial; some critics argue that the amount of duress Mohammed and others are subjected to puts into question the validity of any statements elicited this way. The morality, legality, and effectiveness of these methods are a debate for another time, but in order to talk about highly classified vacuum cleaners, let's take as given that "enhanced interrogation techniques" intentionally aim, in part, to inflict some level of psychological strain on the subjects. Further, there could be some long-term effect on a prisoner's sanity due to such examinations.

It should go without saying that keeping Mohammed sane is pretty important; there's a good chance he can provide value to American security interests going forward. But life as a captured, accused terrorist mastermind isn't all that conducive to maintaining one's sanity. According to a report in the summer of 2013, a decade earlier while Mohammed was an American captive in a secret, CIA-run prison in Romania, he requested an activity intended to keep his brain sharp and occupied between interrogations. According to a person only identified as a "former senior CIA official" by the Associated Press, Mohammed asked to design a vacuum cleaner.

According to the source, Mohammed—who has a mechanical engineering degree from North Carolina A&T State University—wanted permission to start drawing up schematics for a vacuum, which would almost certainly never be built. Why he picked this project is unknown, but his military-assigned lawyer, Jason Wright, told the AP that such a project would be in line with Mohammed's passions; while maintaining a great interest in Islam and the Quran, Mohammed also marvels at modern technology.

The CIA allegedly approved Mohammed's request to start drawing. Further, they allowed him access to some online materials, which helped him design his schematic. So somewhere, in some filing cabinet or data warehouse, there may be plans for an improved home-cleaning system, designed by a person widely characterized as one of history's worst terrorists.

We can't be sure, of course, because the CIA won't confirm or deny what the official told the AP. The CIA responded to a Freedom of Information Act request by claiming that the documents, if they exist, would be highly classified operational files of the agency.

Wright, on the other hand, approached the AP's question with a bit of humor: "It sounds ridiculous, but answering this question, or confirming or denying the very existence of a vacuum-cleaner design, a Swiffer design, or even a design for a better hand towel would apparently expose the U.S. government and its citizens to exceptionally grave danger."

BONUS FACT

Because of Richard Reid and his (thankfully unsuccessful) attempt to blow up an airplane via explosives concealed in his shoe, air travelers in the United States need to take off their shoes when going through airport security and subject them to the package scanners. There's a work-around, though. The Transportation Security Administration (TSA) offers a program called "TSA Precheck," allowing "low-risk travelers to experience expedited, more efficient security screening at participating U.S. airport checkpoints." For a nonrefundable $85 application fee, those who qualify can avoid checking their shoes and belts.

THE BUSH MARKET
THE AFGHAN MERCHANTS REAPING
THE SPOILS OF WAR

Soon after 9/11, American troops went to Kabul, Afghanistan, hoping to stop terrorist cells before they could strike again. Kabul has had an American military presence ever since; for the past eight years, some residents there have felt an enhanced economic effect of the troops' presence.

Which is why, according to the *Washington Post*, some welcome the troops and hope they stay longer.

American soldiers come with guns, tanks, and all sorts of other weaponry, but they also come with other stuff, like snacks and toiletries and various other sundries not typically found in Afghanistan. About eight years ago, a black market of sorts opened in the capital city of this war-torn country. It's named the "Bush Market," after George W. Bush, the president who ordered the troops to Afghanistan originally. The Bush Market has an estimated 600 shops and booths, selling everything from hair dye and acne medicine to Pop-Tarts and other goodies.

While those items are intended for use by American servicemen, they often find themselves in the hands of Afghan vendors—sometimes via trade, but most often by way of theft. As the *Post* explains, while most of the items are stolen property, Afghan authorities leave the market alone unless the Americans ask—and that is rare. The U.S. authorities tend to leave the Bush Market be, unless something sensitive has ended up there. That hasn't happened in about two years.

Despite the presence of armed men loyal to another nation, many of the vendors want the American troops to remain. These entrepreneurs figure that when the soldiers leave, so goes their shops' inventory. One vendor interviewed by the *Post* even believes that reports of a troop pullout have a negative effect on the marketplace's economy, given the uncertainty about the supply of goods.

Until then? As one anonymous merchant told the *Post*, a lot of Afghans are, by the country's standards, getting "very rich doing this."

BONUS FACT

The fact that Pop-Tarts are popular in the Bush Market shouldn't be a surprise—but it should be credited as an American success. In 2001, the United States began airdropping food (in the form of military rations called "meals ready to eat," or MREs) in Afghanistan, hoping to feed some of the millions of people there who were going hungry. Many of the MREs contained Pop-Tarts, which were specifically included to "introduce Afghans to American food," according to the *Baltimore Sun*. Later reports suggested that the United States dropped well over 2 million Pop-Tarts in Afghanistan that year.

MAKING CENTS OF POGS
HOW YESTERDAY'S TOYS BECAME TODAY'S COMBAT CURRENCY

If you grew up in the 1990s in the United States, you probably had a few toys that are hallmarks of your childhood. There were Tamagotchi, the electronic pets you had to take care of or else they'd die; Beanie Babies, a menagerie of collectible stuffed animals; and of course, pogs. Pogs were thin cardboard discs, maybe an inch or two in diameter, often branded with something from the pop culture of the day and used in a schoolyard gambling game of the same name.

But the children of the 1990s grew up, and pogs faded as fads tend to do. The next batch of school children moved on to new trends and hobbies. Pogs, by and large, disappeared.

Then, they came back—in American military bases in Afghanistan, of all places.

After 9/11, tens of thousands of U.S. troops were deployed to Afghanistan, peaking at just over 100,000 troops in the summer of 2011, according to *CBS News*. Not everything provided to the soldiers is rationed, and instead, troops are able to purchase items at what is, effectively, a government-run department store or strip mall. Those shops are run by a division of the Department of Defense called the Army and Air Force Exchange Service (AAFES), which, according to Wikipedia, exists "to provide quality merchandise and services of necessity and convenience to authorized customers at uniform low prices." AAFES also has franchise arrangements with well-known brands such as McDonald's, Burger King, Subway, Starbucks, Home Depot, and video-game retailer GameStop, operating those businesses within or nearby the main store.

Tens of thousand of troops buying stuff means millions of coins in the economy. Unfortunately, that's a problem when the coins come from the United States and the stores are in Afghanistan. Quarters, nickels, pennies, and dimes are heavy in large amounts—$100 worth of quarters, for example, weighs more than five pounds. Shipping all those coins is prohibitive, so instead, during the U.S. presence in Afghanistan, AAFES issued gift certificates. They also looked for a substitute for coins—something that was as convenient as a coin but without the heft—and pogs were the answer. One hundred dollars in twenty-five-cent pogs weighs only about 15 to 20 percent as much as coins. The AAFES issued pogs in five-cent, ten-cent, and twenty-five-cent denominations. There are no one-cent pogs because, let's face it, pennies are annoying enough without being turned into a throwback to a 1990s fad. (AAFES stores round the cost of purchased items to the nearest nickel.)

Just as they were in middle school lunchrooms, pogs have been popular on military bases. Since their introduction in 2001, pogs have become an accepted currency at AAFES stores around the world.

BONUS FACT

The word "pog" was, originally, an acronym. POG was a brand of juice; its name stood for its three core ingredients, passionfruit, orange, and guava. The original pogs were the caps from this blended fruit drink, and the name stuck.

DOUBLE BONUS

One can buy a lot of things at AAFES shops, but one thing a soldier can't buy is the video game *Medal of Honor*. An early version of the game—before it was released—allowed players to assume the role of Taliban fighters taking up arms against Americans. Even though the game's publisher, EA, removed this after public pressure (changing "Taliban" to "Opposing Forces"), the game still won't be found for sale at AAFES-run stores.

PUT UP IN A PARKING LOT
WHERE TO LIVE WHEN YOU REALLY CAN'T GET ENOUGH OF YOUR LOCAL SHOPPING MALL

The Providence Place Mall in Rhode Island is, as malls go, nothing really all that special. As of this writing, there's a Macy's, a Nordstrom, and a J.C. Penney anchoring its hallways. There's a food court, which connects to a movie theater and a Dave and Buster's. On the street level, there's a P.F. Chang's, a CVS, an Uno's Chicago Grill, and a Cheesecake Factory. Pretty generic, down to the paid parking garage.

But in 2007, the last part—the parking garage—had something special: a one-room timeshare apartment.

Make that an illegal one-room timeshare apartment.

When construction of the Providence Place Mall began in the late 1990s, an artist named Michael Townsend, then in his late twenties, lived in the area. According to *Salon*, he wasn't a big fan of the project, seeing it as a taxpayer-funded boondoggle that would change the character and skyline of the neighborhood. In recounting his project a decade later, he'd assert that, during construction, he noticed a sizable region within the confines of the parking garage that was destined to be underused. About five years later, that space would spark an idea.

In 2003, Providence Place began running ads as part of the mall's Christmas shopping season marketing push. One of those ads, in Townsend's words, "featured an enthusiastic female voice talking about how great it would be if you (we) could live at the mall. The central theme of the ad was that the mall not only provided a rich shopping experience but also had all the things that one would need to survive and lead a healthy life." Being a self-described artist, he decided to put that assertion to the test. Over the next few months, he gained access to the space—750 square feet—and converted it into a small apartment.

Townsend would spend up to three weeks at a time living in the apartment, spending those days documenting life as a denizen of the mall. When he wasn't living there—he wasn't homeless, and spent most of the time in a legitimate apartment in a real apartment building—other artists with whom he was friendly took up temporary residence in his secret space. Over the course of the nearly four years of the apartment's existence, a half-dozen or so artists rotated through the space.

All this came to an end after a lightweight sting operation in 2007. Mall security found out about the "dwelling" and, working with Providence police, set up a sting to catch Townsend leaving his unique vacation home. The work Townsend and company had done, to that date, was impressive. While it lacked running water (residents had to use mall bathrooms, and let's just not think about how they bathed), it was otherwise well stocked. The *Boston Globe* reported that the apartment contained "a sectional sofa and love seat, coffee and breakfast tables, chairs, lamps, rugs, paintings, a hutch filled with china, a waffle iron, TV and Sony PlayStation 2." Ironically, the PlayStation wasn't there when Townsend was finally caught; someone had broken into the apartment and stolen it.

The thief who ripped off the PlayStation was never caught. Townsend, for his crime, was given probation.

BONUS FACT

In 2007, having an unauthorized apartment in Providence, Rhode Island, was clearly illegal. But incredibly—and perhaps accidentally—prostitution was not. While revising the state's legal code in 1980, legislators removed the section dealing with prostitution itself while retaining those parts dealing with on-street solicitation, running a brothel, etc. In doing so, they made the act of buying and selling sexual services legal within the state's borders. Some politicians claim that the deletion was an error, but the law wasn't changed back until 2009.

HOT TO SHOP
HOW ONE OF AMERICA'S LARGEST MALLS AVOIDS SCARY UTILITY BILLS

The Mall of America is located in Bloomington, Minnesota, just a few miles outside of Minneapolis/St. Paul. It is enormous. Beyond the nearly 3 million square feet of retail space, the Mall of America is host to Nickelodeon Universe, the largest indoor theme park in the country; the Sea Life Minnesota Aquarium; a mini-golf course; a wedding chapel; and other attractions typically reserved for vacation destinations. At a massive 4.2 million square feet, it's the largest mall in the United States. (The King of Prussia Mall in Pennsylvania has slightly more square footage dedicated to stores than does the Mall of America, but the latter has more total area.) For residents of the Bloomington area, the mall is also a respite from often-harsh weather—from December through February, for example, the average high temperature is below freezing, and residents are regularly greeted with snow.

Yet despite its size and location, the mall's heating bills are low. As in, almost zero.

Construction for the Mall of America began in the summer of 1989 at the site of Metropolitan Stadium, a then-retired baseball and football stadium, which was the home of the Minnesota Twins and Vikings. When constructing the complex, the owners and developers decided that heating the common spaces, especially in the cold winters (nearby St. Paul averages about fifty inches of snow each year) required special attention. Instead of installing a massive central heating system, the mall's owners decided to go green, and, hopefully, save a lot of money in the process.

The mall has more than 1.2 miles of skylights, each bringing in a little bit of sunshine and warming the corridors that connect shops to one another. Then there's the excess heat from all the things being used throughout the mall—escalators, lights, and the roller coaster (yes, the mall has a roller coaster)—which helps keep the mall toasty even during the winter. Most important are the shoppers, tourists, and employees themselves—their body heat means that you'll rarely find a day where the internal temperature of the mall falls below 70 degrees Fahrenheit.

Some stores still have their own heating systems, and many of the entranceways to the mall have heaters as well, but for all the common areas, heat is abundant, thanks to the mall's design and inhabitants. In fact, it may be *too* abundant—at times, all this free heat makes the mall overly warm. It's not uncommon for the air conditioning to be on even during the winter, as particularly busy days may lead to uncomfortably warm conditions inside.

BONUS FACT

You'll not find a lot of air conditioning in Amish communities, whose people are famous for eschewing what most of us would consider modern conveniences. However, among some Ohio-based Amish, solar panels are so common that, as of 2007, you'd find more in use, per-capita, than among any other community in the state. That's because contrary to popular belief, the Amish aren't against using electricity. Rather, according to *Wired*, they "rejected the enticements of the public power grid, deciding they did not want to be too directly linked to, or dependent on, the outside world." Solar panels, to a large degree, come without those dependencies.

THE POTATO FARMER AND THE HARES
HOW SHEEP REVOLUTIONIZED ULTRA-LONG-DISTANCE RUNNING

The Westfield Group owns and operates shopping malls throughout much of the English-speaking world. Two of those malls are in Australia (where Westfield is headquartered) and are situated about 544 miles from one another—there's the Westfield Parramatta in Sydney and the Westfield Doncaster in Melbourne. In 1983, those malls were Westfield's two largest in that nation. Perhaps as a publicity stunt, their parent company organized a race between the two sites. The Westfield Sydney-to-Melbourne Ultramarathon started in late April. As one would expect, most of the entrants were young but seasoned long- and ultra-long-distance runners. Within the circles of those who follow such things, they were household names.

Five days, fifteen hours, and four minutes after the runners took off, the winner crossed the finish line. His name was Cliff Young. He was a potato farmer who ran funny, had fallen miles behind the competition on the first day, and, oh yeah, was sixty-one years old.

He won by ten hours.

To be fair, Young had been running all of his life; he just hadn't been doing so competitively. Even at age sixty, he was working and living on the family farm on which he grew up. Potatoes were the major crop there, but the 2,000-acre farm was also home to a 2,000-strong herd of sheep. As he explained in various media reports, growing up, his family couldn't afford tractors or horses. When storms came to the region, rounding up the sheep therefore became a major ordeal—and Young had to do it himself, by foot. He claimed to run around, herding sheep, for two or three days straight—often while wearing rainboots. Endurance like that, he correctly believed, gave him a huge advantage over the other runners.

But when the race came, it didn't start off well. Young didn't run with long strides like most of the other runners, instead shuffling his feet over very short distances, a movement that was more of a waddle than a step. Most of the runners left him in the dust. By the time the race was eighteen hours old and racers went to get their typical six hours of sleep, Young was so far off the lead that he was at best a curiosity and at worst a punch line.

Six hours later, the other runners woke up to find that Young hadn't stopped to sleep and was now well in the lead.

It's unclear how much he slept over the five-plus-day run— by some reports, Young didn't sleep at all—but however much it was, it wasn't much. Young finished well in first place because he spent a lot more time running (and less time sleeping) than his competition. He attributed his endurance to his experience chasing down the sheep and, counterintuitively to those watching and participating in the race, his funky-looking running style.

And it turns out that may actually have mattered. Young's running style, now called the "Young Shuffle," is commonly believed to require less energy than other forms of running, making it an attractive option for ultramarathoners, including a few subsequent winners of the Sydney-to-Melbourne race in years after Young's win.

BONUS FACT

The world record for most time awake without sleep? 264 hours, according to *Scientific American*. The record was set in 1965 by a seventeen-year-old who stayed awake for roughly eleven days as part of a science fair experiment.

THE WALK MAN
THE MOST PEDESTRIAN OF SPORTS

Walking is a pretty fundamental method of locomotion for people—almost all of us can do it and do it often. It is also something we take for granted, hardly giving it a second thought. Why would we? While walking may separate us from many other animals, it's so commonplace that we don't think of it as anything special.

Compare it to the requirements of today's great athletic competitions. Baseball, basketball, football, tennis, and soccer players run. If you play ice hockey, you skate. Gymnasts seem to fly. There are cyclists, swimmers, and even people who dance while trying to punch each other unconscious, all in furtherance of athletic accolades and often in front of cheering crowds. In each of these sports, there are heroes, from Babe Ruth and Michael Jordan to Michael Phelps and Muhammad Ali.

No one ever earned fame for winning a walking competition. Except for a guy named Edward Payson Weston, that is.

Weston was born in 1839 in Rhode Island, and in 1860 he made a bet that would change his life forever (and the world of sports temporarily). He wagered that Abraham Lincoln would lose the upcoming presidential election, agreeing to attend Lincoln's inauguration if he lost the bet. The wrinkle was that Weston would have to walk to Washington for the event, which was particularly problematic because Weston lived in Boston, nearly 500 miles away.

Lincoln won the election and on February 22, 1861, Weston started walking. The trip took him ten days and ten hours, and the weather didn't cooperate—he had to battle through snow, ice, and rain, making the grueling trip even less of a walk in the park. He barely slept, he ate while he walked (which was hard to do in the days before granola bars and ziplock bags), but he managed to arrive on time for the festivities in Washington. His trek drew media attention, and he became a minor celebrity. He even got to meet Lincoln; as Wikipedia notes, he received "a congratulatory handshake from the new president."

Weston had found his calling and kept on walking. As retold by ESPN's Grantland, "In 1867, he became a household name by walking from Portland, Maine, to Chicago in 26 days, 1,200 miles along the post road. Weston was greeted by massive crowds everywhere he went; newspaper writers around the country worked themselves into a froth debating the merits of the undertaking." His efforts, defying common sense and the elements, ushered in a nationwide interest in a new sport called "pedestrianism"— competitive walking.

For the remainder of the 1800s, pedestrianism continued to grow throughout the United States and even found significant popularity in Great Britain. Some races were city-to-city jaunts, at times taking weeks, but the big commercial value lay in "six-day races" at arenas such as Madison Square Garden. Matthew Algeo, author of the book *Pedestrianism*, which chronicles the sport, explained in an interview with NPR that competitors would walk around a track, typically an eighth of a mile long, from midnight Monday morning until midnight the next Saturday evening. The rules varied, but in many cases, whoever walked farthest won; at other times, the competition was to see who could last the longest without collapsing. (In all cases, competitive walkers were afforded a brief sleep break each day, but nowhere near eight hours of it.) These races attracted thousands upon thousands of fans, spectators, and gamblers, each willing to pay for a ticket and various concessions.

In the sport's heyday, Weston was a household name on both sides of the pond. He dedicated most of his life to the sport, even as its popularity waned. In 1913—then age seventy-three or seventy-four—Weston walked from New York City to Minneapolis in fifty-one days. The trip was more than 1,500 miles; that's thirty miles a day.

Competitive walking waned around the turn of the twentieth century. It almost entirely disappeared after the invention of the car (although the much-less-popular racewalking persisted for a time), which, in a cruel form of irony, also robbed Weston of his notable skill. In 1927, well after he retired from his now-dead sport, Weston was hit by a taxicab. He would never walk again, competitively or otherwise, and was confined to a wheelchair. He passed away two years later.

BONUS FACT

Walking can also be a job in and of itself in modern times—notably in Tehran, Iran. Because of Tehran's traffic and pollution concerns, the government only allows cars to take to the roads on alternate days—cars with license plates ending in odd numbers on odd-numbered days and even plates on even days. Some drivers, wanting to get around the law, hire people to walk behind their cars in the traffic-heavy areas, obscuring their license plates and helping the drivers avoid traffic tickets.

DABBAWALA
HOW TO BRING YOUR LUNCH TO WORK IN INDIA

Imagine a man on a bicycle carrying two dozen or so metallic cylindrical containers, each of which resembles a small beer keg or a transportation capsule for toxic waste. The containers—most often made of tin or aluminum—are called *dabbas*. There are 4,500 to 5,000 dabbawalas riding around every alley and street of Mumbai, India, every day, even during monsoon season, often traveling long distances. Collectively, the dabbawalas traffic as many as 200,000 dabbas each day.

But don't worry. They're delivering lunch.

Translated literally, *dabbawala* means "box person" or "one who carries a box." A *dabba* is a box—in this case, a bit of a misnomer because the "boxes" used are clearly cylinders—while *wala* is a suffix for one who does something with the item. In this sense, a dabbawala is simply a food delivery guy, which sounds like a rather pedestrian (pardon the unintentional reverse pun) occupation. But in Mumbai, being a dabbawala isn't just a job—it's a skilled trade all to itself. And a highly successful one at that.

The dabbawala trade began in the mid-to-late 1800s during the British Raj, the British rule of India. Many Britons who came to India did not enjoy the local cuisine and wanted to eat a more familiar lunch (called "tiffin") at work. However, their offices did not have kitchens, and carrying a lunch was either too cumbersome or beneath the generally aristocratic colonial rulers. It became necessary to transport lunches from the homes of British colonists to their places of work, and a cottage industry cropped up. By 1890, a 100-person delivery company was running much of the lunch delivery business in the area, and over the course of the next half-century or so, the dabbawala industry formed a union, now known as the Nutan Mumbai Tiffin Box Suppliers Trust. Today, although the British Raj is long gone, the business is still growing; in 2007, the *New York Times* reported that the dabbawala industry was increasing at 5–10 percent annually.

Why is business so good? Mumbai's traffic can be nightmarishly bad, making the trip from suburbs to city by car unworkable for most people. Taking the train is a better option, but that makes it difficult to carry items, and the commute is so long that lunch would have to be prepared the night before. A small but meaningful percentage of Mumbai office workers choose to let the network of dabbawalas handle the lunch part. Each day, one delivery person picks up lunch later in the morning, bicycles it and others along its route to the train, and another dabbawala transports the lunch the rest of the way. For 450 rupees per month—that's about $8.25—workers can get their home-cooked meals brought to them with nearly 100 percent reliability.

Yes, nearly 100 percent. The dabbawalas, who are often illiterate, navigate the roadways of Mumbai with incredible efficiency. As the *Guardian* noted, "*Forbes* awarded the humble dabba-wallahs [*sic*] a 6 Sigma performance rating, a term used in quality assurance if the percentage of correctness is 99.9999999 or more. In other words, for every six million tiffins delivered, only one fails to arrive. This error rate means in effect that a tiffin goes astray only once every two months." In 2011, when the team from the television show

Top Gear tried to beat a dabbawala delivery service by using a car instead of the train, they failed miserably.

The dabbawalas themselves earn 8,000 to 10,000 rupees per month (roughly $150–$175), or about 100,000–120,000 rupees annually. This is much higher than the per-capita income in India—about 53,333 rupees (about $975) per year—but that's not enough, many claim. Due to the higher cost of living in the Mumbai area, combined with recent upticks in inflation, the dabbawala union recently requested taxi-operator permits for 2,000 of its 5,000 members.

BONUS FACT

If Guy de Maupassant, a famous nineteenth-century French writer, wanted his lunch delivered by dabbawala (leaving aside that there are none in Paris, certainly not when Maupassant was alive), he would have had them deliver the cooked meals to the base of Paris's Eiffel Tower. Not because he liked the food at the Tower's restaurant. The Tower, completed in 1889, was not immediately well received by many, and especially not Maupassant. As the *New York Times* noted, Maupassant "saw the tower as an affront to his nation's proud cultural heritage and dined regularly in its restaurant because that was the one spot in Paris from which he didn't have to look upon 'this giant and disgraceful skeleton.'"

FLUSHED WITH LOVE
THE THRONE THAT COMES WITH
A LICENSE TO MARRY

The requirements for obtaining a marriage license in the state of New York are rather boring. Each person has to be at least eighteen years old or have parental consent (and in no case will the state issue a marriage license to someone under the age of fourteen). Certain close relatives can't marry, and people who are currently married to other people are similarly ineligible to marry someone else. You have to fork over $40. But it's pretty straightforward, as you'd expect. By requiring that the grooms first send in a picture of their commode before issuing a marriage license, the government is incentivizing the start of a cultural change via infrastructure improvements.

But to participate in a particular marriage ceremony in the Madhya Pradesh, a state in India, you need to prove something else. The groom needs to show that his domicile comes with a toilet.

Really.

In early 2013, Madhya Pradesh officials conducted a mass marriage ceremony to provide a way for women from poor families to wed their would-be grooms. It's a program that has been around since 2006 or 2007. The recent ceremony attracted just under 200 couples to the proverbial (but in this case, nonexistent) altar, and the program has seen nearly 2,000 poor couples enter into marriage this way in about a year's time. And the state is using it as an opportunity to fix another problem.

According to the World Toilet Organization—yes, there's a World Toilet Organization (and it's actually a pretty serious charity)—there are about 2.5 billion people without access to a functioning private toilet. Most of them live in developing regions and are very poor, and the fledgling families in Madhya Pradesh are no exception. A recent survey suggests that half of all Indian households lack a toilet, which is a major public health issue. As *Fast Company* points out, improperly disposed-of fecal matter is the largest killer of children across the world, claiming over 1.4 million young lives a year. According to a 2007 report by Bloomberg, India accumulates as much as 100,000 tons of human excrement in fields each day.

So far, we don't know whether the toilets-for-marriage-licenses program will have an effect on the problem. But the problem is significant enough to warrant this otherwise absurd-sounding requirement.

BONUS FACT

Ghana is looking at another way of dealing with the same problem, but their solution doesn't involve marriage. It involves recycling. According to *GOOD*, "fecal sludge" (their words) may be able to be used as an industrial fuel—basically, a (rather gross) biodiesel. The theory is, if that happens, markets will form to purchase the sludge before it becomes an everyday pollutant, thereby creating the financial incentive necessary to prevent haphazard dumping of latrines. The initiative has serious support behind it—it is backed by the Bill and Melinda Gates Foundation.

UNMOUNTAIN MAN
HOW FAR CAN YOU GO WITH A HAMMER, CHISEL,
AND SOME NAILS?

In 1992, Canadian singer Celine Dion released a single titled "Love Can Move Mountains." The song, which peaked at #36 on the *Billboard* U.S. Hot 100 chart and at #8 overall on Canada's equivalent, probably should not have its title taken literally. But no one bothered to tell that to an Indian laborer named Dashrath Manjhi.

Manjhi hails from a small village in the northeast of India near the city of Gaya. Sometime in the 1950s or 1960s—sources differ on the exact date—his wife, Falguni Devi, fell ill and required medical care. According to DNA India, between Manjhi and Devi's village and the nearest hospital stood mountainous terrain, with no road running through it. The couple traveled around the mountains—a forty-five-mile (seventy-five-kilometer) trek—but by then, it was too late. Devi died, and Manjhi thereafter committed himself to making sure no one befell a similar fate. So he started tunneling.

For the next two decades, Manjhi worked day and night, carving a road from his village through the mountain; according to the *Hindustan Times*, he used only a hammer, chisel, and nails. By the time he completed the project in the 1980s (again, sources differ on the end date), Manjhi had dug a tunnel 360 feet long, twenty-five feet high, and thirty feet wide. Residents of his community could, due to his tireless work, now get through the mountain, which was no small victory. Manjhi's road cut the required travel distance from his area to the neighboring one dramatically, from a forty-five-mile distance to only about half a mile.

Unfortunately, that was only part of the job. Connecting the mountain pass to the main roadway required a public works project, and while the local government originally agreed to fund that, the project was put on hold in 2007. Manjhi died later that year and received a state funeral in honor of his work, and it is unclear if work on the road has resumed. But another project, perhaps more fitting, is underway. According to the Indian Express, the local government is building a hospital, named after Manjhi, near his village.

BONUS FACT

There's a mountain about thirty-five miles north of Melbourne, Australia, which was first summited in 1824. From its peak, the explorers expected to be able to see Port Phillip Bay, the body of water just to Melbourne's south, but when they arrived at the top, they learned that the tree cover prevented such a majestic sight. They named the mountain after their experience, and today, if you'd like, you can go for a hike on what has since been called Mount Disappointment.

DORMANT AND TIRED
THE VOLCANIC ERUPTION THAT WASN'T

Kruzof Island is in the North Pacific Ocean, one of many Alaskan islands that run down what would otherwise be the Canadian coastline. It's not too far from the state capital, Juneau. Kruzof Island is home to Mount Edgecumbe, a dormant volcano stretching about 3,200 feet to its summit. Mount Edgecumbe is a tourist attraction—it makes for a manageable hike and is generally safe. The most difficult part about climbing the mountain is getting to it in the first place—Kruzof Island does not have a permanent human population, and therefore there are no regular transports to the mountain. The closest town, Sitka, Alaska, is on a nearby island. To climb Edgecumbe, one typically leaves from Sitka.

In general, placing a city near a volcano is a bad idea, but Edgecumbe has been dormant for millennia—its last known eruption was more than four thousand years ago. But in 1974, the town of Sitka got a scare. Edgecumbe, apparently, started to awaken from its long slumber. On the first day of April in that year, a plume of black smoke rose from the top of the mountain. Conditions in the area were unusually clear, and people from Sitka could easily see the now-festering volcano. Was Edgecumbe no longer dormant?

The Coast Guard went to check, dispatching a helicopter to fly over the volcano's crater and check for—well, who knows? What the helicopter pilot saw, though, was not an eruption. Rather, it was a message in the snow, spray painted in large black letters:

"APRIL FOOL"

Sitka was the target of an extravagant prank.

The prankster's name was Oliver Bickar, better known as Porky to his friends and family. The middle-aged man came up with the idea in 1971—three years earlier!—and started preparing. He collected dozens of old tires in an airplane hangar and waited. The conditions were near perfect on, coincidentally, April Fool's Day 1974. He convinced some friends (and a helicopter pilot) to help him transport his collection of tires to the mountain's summit, douse them all in kerosene, and light them on fire. He even went to the trouble of getting clearance for his prank from the FAA and local police—just to make sure that they didn't get arrested, and to make sure local officials could prevent a panic outbreak. (They forgot to or neglected to inform the Coast Guard.)

Not only did Bickar not get in trouble for his prank, but, as recounted by the website The Museum of Hoaxes, he actually got a lot of good press about it and positive reactions from locals. Even a Coast Guard admiral congratulated Porky on a prank well pulled.

BONUS FACT

Juneau, Alaska, is only accessible by air or sea—all cars and trucks in the city are brought in on barges or ferries. Road construction and maintenance is expensive, given the environment of the area. None of Juneau's roads leave the city.

THE PRIDE OF GEORGIA TECH
THE BIG MAN ON CAMPUS (WHOM YOU'LL NEVER SEE IN CLASS)

In 1931, George P. Burdell graduated from Georgia Institute of Technology (better known as Georgia Tech) with a BS in Ceramic Engineering. A few years later, Burdell received a master's degree from this same institution. One of the college yearbooks lists him as a member of the basketball team and his engagement was announced in the major Atlanta paper, the *Atlanta Journal-Constitution*. He'd leave Georgia Tech soon after, entering military service in World War II—for a time he was listed as being part of the air force, flying a dozen missions over Europe. But Georgia Tech was Burdell's home. He'd return to the school, enrolling in countless other classes, and remained active in the campus community, writing letters to the editor of the college paper; he is so ubiquitous at football games that he is regularly singled out by the public address announcer. There is even a store in the student center named after him. At Georgia Tech, George P. Burdell is a popular fellow.

He is also entirely fake.

In 1927, William Edgar Smith was admitted to Georgia Tech—but, accidentally, received two enrollment forms. While most people would simply throw away the second, Smith decided to pull a prank, enrolling a second, fake person as well as himself. Smith combined the names of his high school principal (George P. Butler) and the maiden name of a family friend (Burdell) and came up with the amalgam for his prank. From that point forward, Smith had Burdell mirror his actions at Georgia Tech. If Smith enrolled for a class, so would Burdell. When Smith turned in an assignment, he'd turn in a slightly adjusted one for Burdell. When Smith took an exam, he'd do so twice—one for him, one for his "ghost." Burdell graduated and is an official alumnus, even though he never existed.

Other students have been carrying on Smith's legacy ever since, mass-enrolling him in classes despite the university's best efforts. (Multiple times the university upgraded its systems to prevent Burdell from appearing on the class rolls; the students proved savvier, defeating these attempts time and time again.) Burdell's inclusion in the air force, on the George Tech basketball team, and everywhere else is the byproduct of an organically developed ruse over the course of nearly a century—with no end in sight.

BONUS FACT

As old as the Burdell hoax is, it may not be the longest-running one. In late 1917, American journalist H.L. Mencken wrote a column in the *New York Evening Mail* titled, "A Neglected Anniversary," retelling the unsung history of the bathtub. Mencken's history of the washbasin was undisclosed fiction, alleging (among other things) that President Millard Fillmore popularized the bathtub in the United States by installing one in the White House in 1850. While made up, some of these "facts" have been cited as true as recently as 2008 (in a Kia commercial, of all things).

LOST AND FOUND
THE MISSING PERSON LIVING IN SAVANNAH

Benjaman Kyle is missing.

Benjaman Kyle also lives in Savannah, Georgia. If you had his address, you could go visit him, and he'd be there, doing whatever he does each day.

But if you go to the Doe Network, an organization that helps locate missing people, he'll be there. In fact, his case file is 1007UMGA. But unlike everyone else in the Doe Network's database, Kyle is not in there because no one knows *where* he is—rather, it's because no one knows *who* he is.

On August 31, 2004, Kyle was found unconscious behind a Burger King, near a dumpster. He was naked, beaten, and bitten by fire ants. His wallet and ID were gone—as was much of his memory. He could not recall any of the events of the past twenty years. He did not know what his name was, where he was from, and did not even recognize his own face. The mystery man adopted the name "Benjaman Kyle" in part because the initials—B.K.—are also Burger King's. He believes that his true first name is "Benjaman" (with the curious spelling) and therefore uses that name, but there is little to no evidence that he is correct.

His memory is shattered, but over the course of the past few years, he and others have pieced together some likely information about his life before the summer of 2004. He recognizes certain landmarks from Indianapolis, Indiana, which others have used to conclude that he lived in the area sometime in the late 1950s to early 1960s. His spotty but detailed recollection of certain parts of the University of Colorado, Boulder, library and other locations around the campus strongly suggests that he attended the university in the late 1970s or early 1980s. Together, these pieces of information suggest he's approximately sixty years old.

Kyle also has extensive knowledge of how the restaurant and food preparation business works, and he remembers how to operate the machinery. (While he lost his memory, many of his acquired skills remain intact.) Unfortunately, he cannot remember his Social Security number—until recently, he was unable to get an ID card issued and therefore, unable to gain employment. That changed in 2011, when a local government agency helped him get a government-issued ID, and he later found work as a dishwasher.

BONUS FACT

Ben Pridmore of England is a memory champion. He can memorize the order of multiple decks of playing cards in a matter of minutes and once memorized the order of twenty-seven decks of cards—1,404 cards total—with only an hour of study. Most incredibly, Pridmore once committed to memory the correct order of a single deck of cards—in twenty-six seconds.

INVISIBLE CHILDREN
WHEN 7 MILLION KIDS VANISHED FROM THE GOVERNMENT'S EYE

In the spring of 1987—if you ask government accountants, at least—roughly 7 million American children vanished without a trace. Seven million, gone. According to a report by the Scripps Howard News Service in 1990, at least 400 people were being investigated for crimes relating to the disappearance of these children.

The criminal conspiracy of the century? Hardly. Just some garden-variety tax fraud.

The U.S. federal income tax law is a muddled, 70,000-plus-page mess of rules and requirements. One of the better-known rules, though, is that parents can claim their children as "dependents," since the children rely on the adults for sustenance, shelter, and basically everything else. Claiming your children as dependents will save you some money when tax season comes around. (The allowance is so well known that it's not uncommon for obstetricians to half-jokingly tell expectant parents that they're better off having their new arrival come before the first of the upcoming year, so the child counts in the current tax year.) The quick math takeaway: more children equals less taxes.

But if your budget-balancing strategy is to have more kids, well, that's a pretty horrible idea. Kids are expensive—they cost more than the tax money they'll save you, easily. So some people, apparently, decided to lie to the government instead. Thousands of people wrote down that they had children, getting some relief from Uncle Sam in the process, and just pretended that the kids existed. Hey, free money, right?

That all changed when Congress passed the Tax Reform Act of 1986. One of the provisions required that if you claimed a person over the age of five as a dependent, you had to include his or her Social Security number on your tax filing. Just like that, 7 million children formerly claimed as dependents no longer were.

While some of those children actually existed—perhaps the parents hadn't, wouldn't, or couldn't apply for a Social Security number for them—there's good reason to believe that in many cases fraud was the order of the day. The IRS commissioned a study to find out where all the children had gone, and the results were startling. At least 60,000 families claimed four or more dependent children in 1986 and then, in 1987, claimed none at all. Even more egregious: more than 11,000 tax filers claimed at least seven (seven!) fewer children than they had the year prior. Nearly 5 percent of those 11,000 faced criminal charges for what constituted obvious fraud.

Most of the "missing" children were, therefore, never found. But the IRS found something else—$2.8 billion in additional taxes collected, compared to the prior year.

BONUS FACT

In the state of New York (as of 2013), food items sold for at-home consumption are not subject to sales tax, while food sold for eating at, say, a restaurant, is taxed. Sometimes, it's obvious which side of the line your purchase falls on, but that's not always the case. Take, for example, bagels. As *USA Today* reported, if you were to buy a bagel or two at a local bakery, you'd pay no tax. But if you asked that bagel to be sliced for you? Prepare to pony up an extra 8 percent. An "altered" bagel—and slicing it constitutes an alteration—is assumed to be intended for on-premises consumption.

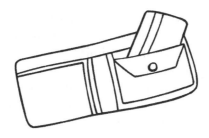

REPETITIVE NUMBERS
WHY A LOT OF PEOPLE THOUGHT THEY HAD THE SAME ID NUMBER

Social Security has been part of the American economic and political landscape since its inception in August 1935. As part of the New Deal, President Franklin Delano Roosevelt signed into law the Social Security Act, which aimed at alleviating poverty among senior citizens, as at the time, roughly 50 percent of them were living below the poverty line. Social Security created a tax on payrolls, the revenue from which would be used to pay monthly benefits to seniors, as well as a lump-sum payment upon death.

In order to create this system, the federal government created Social Security Numbers (SSN)—unique identifiers that allowed the system to track all the collections and payments. Unfortunately, as we know today, identity theft is rampant, in part because the SSN system does little to protect our numbers from becoming available to anyone. Take the case of Hilda Schrader Whitcher, whose SSN was used by 5,755 people in the year 1943, alone.

But Whitcher was not the victim of identity theft thousands of times over. Rather, her number was given out in wallets.

In 1938, just a few years after the Social Security Act became law, a wallet manufacturer decided to include sample cards in their leather products, encouraging purchasers to use their new wallets to carry around Social Security cards. (As it turns out, this was bad advice; the Social Security Administration advises that you not carry around anything with your SSN on it.) The cards were labeled with the word "specimen" so as to not confuse the wallet's new owner into thinking that the card provided contained a true SSN. Whitcher was the secretary of the executive who came up with the fake-card idea, and it was her number—078-05-1120—that was emblazoned on the sample card.

The wallet was a retail success, finding distribution across the country when Woolworth, at the time the biggest single retail chain in the nation, decided to carry it. Unfortunately, as Whitcher would later find out, thousands of people began using her number as their own—sparking all sorts of inconveniences for her, including a visit from the FBI. In total, roughly 40,000 people have claimed SSN 078-05-1120 as their own since the fake cards were first printed. This misuse went on for decades. As recently as 1977—nearly forty years after it was first placed on sample cards—Whitcher's number was still being used by about a dozen people.

While Whitcher and Woolworth learned the "do not make documents with fake SSNs, even as samples" rule the hard way, another organization did not heed their lesson. In 1962, this organization printed a pamphlet aimed at answering common questions about how the Social Security system works, and on the front of the pamphlet was a picture of a card with a sample number—219-09-9999. That number was, of course, erroneously adopted by confused pensioners and employees alike. But the embarrassing part?

The organization that published the pamphlet was the Social Security Administration.

BONUS FACT

The first person to receive Social Security benefits was a lady named Ida May Fuller, who retired in 1939 at the age of sixty-five and received her first check—for $22.54—on January 31, 1940. Fuller had worked for three years under the Social Security system, so she had made some contributions to the overall fund, but only $24.75 worth. She came out ahead by the time she cashed her second benefits check—the second of very, very many. Fuller lived to be 100, passing away on January 31, 1975, thirty-five years to the day she received that $22.54. Her total lifetime Social Security benefits? $22,888.92.

THE BIRTHDAY PROBLEM
HOW TO USE BIRTHDAYS TO WIN BAR BETS

Let's make a couple of assumptions. First, let's assume that birthdays are randomly distributed—given enough people, you'll have roughly the same number born on, say, December 13 as you will on November 22 or April 14. (As it turns out, this isn't quite true.) Second, let's assume that February 29—Leap Day—doesn't exist. (Also untrue.) Finally, let's assume that everyone uses the 365-day Gregorian calendar. (Mostly true.) Got it? Nothing too controversial.

Say you walk into an empty auditorium. A minute or so later, someone else walks in. Given the previous assumptions, there's a 1 in 365 chance (0.27 percent) that this person shares your birthday. A second person walks in a minute or two later. The odds of you sharing a birthday with either jump to about 0.55 percent. A third and a fourth and—you get the idea. Only when the 253rd person walks in do you have a 50 percent chance of having the same birthday as someone else in the room. It isn't person 182 or 183, because some of the first 200-something people may share birthdays with each other. So a birthday shared with person 254 (including you) should make intuitive sense—or, at least, not be terribly shocking.

But let's look at it a different way. Again, you start off in an empty auditorium and again, every few minutes, someone new comes into the room. Instead of wondering if *you* share a birthday with anyone else in the room, let's make this about *everyone* in the room. Let's ask: "Do any two people in the room share a birthday?" The math starts off the same—with two people, there's still a 1-in-365 chance. The third person? The odds aren't 0.55 percent anymore—now, there's a 0.82 percent chance that anyone in the group matches someone else. Yes, you could share a birthday with either of the other two people—that's the 0.55 percent—but they could share a birthday with each other, too. That's where the extra percentage boost comes from.

How many people before we hit a 50 percent chance that any two share a birthday? Twenty-three. Not 230. Twenty-three. Here's a graph:

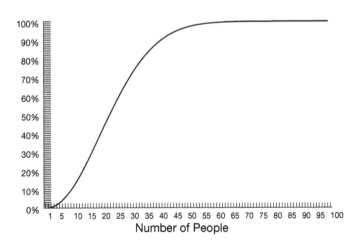

Probability of Two or More Sharing a Birthday

The odds go up very quickly because each new person can match every other person in the room, and as the number of people in the room grows, the gains are huge. At fifty-seven people, there is just over a 99 percent chance of any two people in the room sharing a birthday. And, in case you are wondering, at 124 people, there is less than a 0.0000000001 percent chance of there *not* being a match. That's one in one hundred trillion.

BONUS FACT

Of course, birthdays aren't random. Some months have more births than others, for reasons one can imagine (and you'd almost certainly be correct). The days of the week should be random—but, at least in the United States, they aren't. Why not? As BabyCenter explains, Tuesdays and then Mondays have the highest number of births, because hospitals try not to schedule C-sections or induce labor on the weekends.

HAPPY BIRTHDAY®
WHY RESTAURANTS HAVE SILLY BIRTHDAY SONGS

The song is iconic: "*Happy birthday to you*," twice. "*Happy birthday*" (again) followed by the birthday boy or girl's name. And again, to close, "*Happy birthday to you*." *The Guinness Book of World Records* (as of 1998) says that "Happy Birthday" is the most recognizable English-language song in existence, followed by "For He's a Jolly Good Fellow" and then "Auld Lang Syne." But unlike the second and third most recognizable English songs, "Happy Birthday" has another distinction: It is under copyright.

In 1893, two sisters from Kentucky, Mildred and Patty Hill, composed a song called "Good Morning to All." The lyrics—"Good morning to you / good morning to you / good morning dear children / good morning to all"—are foreign to modern ears. However, the melody the sisters used for the song was that used in "Happy Birthday."

Sometime over the next few decades, that tune was wed to the lyrics we all know. Nobody knows exactly who wrote the stanza we all sing regularly—depending on whom you ask, "Happy Birthday" may be by the same two sisters or it may not have been written for twenty years thereafter. What we do know: the lyrics appeared in a 1924 book, as a second stanza following the original one of "Good Morning to All." The song appeared in a series of other contexts soon after. In 1935, the company that originally published "Good Morning to All"—working with the Hills' sister Jessica—copyrighted "Happy Birthday."

Today, the rights are owned by Warner Music Group. Warner continues to enforce the copyright insofar as public and/or for-profit performances are concerned. (Don't worry about singing it at a private family gathering.) Enforcement of the copyright netted the company $2 million in royalties in 2008 alone, and apparently, the Walt Disney Company paid $5,000 to use the song in a ride at Epcot Center a few decades ago.

Some take steps to avoid the fees. For example, some filmmakers substitute "For He's a Jolly Good Fellow" when "Happy Birthday" would otherwise be more appropriate. Perhaps absurdly, in an effort to skirt paying royalties to Warner Music some chain restaurants instruct servers to sing atypical birthday songs when guests celebrate at their establishments.

"Happy Birthday" was originally scheduled to enter the public domain in 1991, but a pair of copyright extension laws in the United States (not specific to this song) extended its copyright another four decades. Absent other extensions, the song will enter public domain in the United States in 2030 and in the European Union at the close of 2016.

BONUS FACT

In 1963, an artist named Harvey Ball created the iconic yellow smiley face. He did it as a freelancer on behalf of the company now known as Hanover Insurance—but neither he nor the company ever registered the artwork with the copyright or trademark offices. Ball made a total of $45 from his creation—the fee Hanover paid him for the work.

A FANTASTIC COPY
WHY HOLLYWOOD MADE A MOVIE THEY NEVER WANTED YOU TO WATCH

The Fantastic Four—Mr. Fantastic, the Invisible Woman, the Human Torch, and the Thing—originally appeared in an eponymous 1961 comic book released by Marvel Comics. They were popular for decades and, in 2005, 20th Century Fox released a movie about the heroic quartet, which earned over $330 million at the box office with a $100 million budget. A sequel, *Fantastic Four: Rise of the Silver Surfer*, hit theaters two years later, earning $290 million at the box office with a budget of $130 million. Despite the apparently massive amounts of money these movies made, studio execs were disappointed and put the franchise on hold for nearly a decade. (A rebooted series was planned for 2015 release.)

There's another Fantastic Four movie—but you've probably never seen it. Technically speaking, it came out in 1994, but it never hit theaters nor had a home video release. To make matters even stranger, the film's producers didn't care at all. In fact, they were probably happy.

In the 1980s, Marvel Comics wasn't yet set up to produce movies. The company ended up licensing some of their characters to various movie studios—that's why Spider-Man movies are produced by Sony and the X-Men films are distributed by 20th Century Fox. (Marvel has retained some rights—most notably to Iron Man, Captain America, the Incredible Hulk, and the rest of the Avengers—and will regain the rights to their licensed characters at some point, but probably not too soon.) The Fantastic Four were one of the franchises licensed out during that boom period. In 1983, a production company named Neue Constantin purchased the option to create a Fantastic Four movie for what is rumored to be about $250,000.

That option was set to expire on December 31, 1992, and as that date approached, Neue Constantin was nowhere close to having a summer blockbuster ready—a week before that date, they hadn't even started production. Neue Constantin approached Marvel for an extension, but was rebuffed. So they came up with another idea: Make a really terrible movie on the cheap.

The agreement between Marvel and Neue Constantin allowed the latter to retain the rights to the characters so long as they produced a movie before the date in question. The theory behind this ancillary right makes sense—if the production company makes a smash hit, they should be able to produce a sequel. Neue Constantin, many would later argue, used this as a loophole. In September 1992, they brought on a low-budget producer who could quickly churn out a Fantastic Four movie with a budget of only $1 million, chump change by industry standards. Production began on December 28, 1992, a few days before the deadline, and wrapped a month later. The film was slated to come out in late 1993 or 1994 but was scrapped before it hit theaters.

The reasons why are unclear. Stan Lee, the legend behind Marvel, claims that Neue Constantin never intended to release the film—by simply creating the movie, the production company was able to maintain its hold on the Fantastic Four franchise for years to come. Neue Constantin's executives tell another story, asserting that Marvel executive Avi Arad caught wind of the low-budget flick and, wanting to protect the Fantastic Four brand, bought all the rights and ordered all copies—including the film negatives—destroyed. (If true, he failed; two decades later, you can find a bootlegged copy on YouTube.)

Either way, Neue Constantin came out ahead. The company retained the rights to the Final Four franchise. If you look at the credits for both the 2005 and 2007 Fantastic Four films, you'll see the name "Constantin Film"—Neue Constantin's new name—as one of the studios involved in the productions.

BONUS FACT

On November 17, 1978, on the heels of the box office success of *Star Wars*, CBS aired the first official *Star Wars* spinoff, called "The Star Wars Holiday Special." The ninety-seven-minute show was a weird variety show–style disaster, which was nearly universally panned. In response to the negative reviews, the powers that be decided to never re-air it or release it on home video. Thanks to the magic of the Internet, though, you can find a copy online pretty easily. (But, as someone who has seen it, take my word for it: Don't bother.)

THE KEEPER OF THE HOLOCRON
THE GUY WHO WATCHES STAR WARS FOR A LIVING

When the first Star Wars movie, *A New Hope*, debuted in 1977, it introduced a complex universe of planets, species, religions, and ethos, which quickly expanded well beyond the 121-minute-long story of Luke Skywalker's triumph over the Death Star. The original trilogy was later unfortunately expanded by a series of three "prequels." And there were the cartoons. And toys. And books. And video games. And everything else.

With all of that content come a lot of details—different parts of the back stories of dozens of different species and hundreds of different characters, for example. When things get too complicated, many other brands "reboot" their universes, discarding most of the details and retaining just the broad strokes. But those at LucasFilm in control of Star Wars chose a different tactic. They hired Leland Chen.

He's the Keeper of the Holocron.

Really. It says that right on his LinkedIn profile.

Holocrons are, appropriately, fictional devices from the Star Wars universe itself. Wookieepedia—that's not a typo, but the name of an unofficial Wikipedia-like encyclopedia of Star Wars information—defines a Holocron as an "organic crystal-lattice device which stored phenomenal quantities of data guarded by the device's gatekeeper." In other words, it's a high-tech library from a long time ago in a galaxy far, far away. The real-life equivalent of the Holocron is the database of Star Wars info that Chen administers—he'd be considered the gatekeeper, if you wanted to mirror the lexicon.

Chen was hired by LucasFilm in January 2000 to create this database. (His official title is "Continuity Database Administrator," according to a *Wired* profile.) As he explained on the official Star Wars blog before he joined the company, LucasFilm had binders full of information about the universe, but it was quickly getting unwieldy and therefore difficult for licensees and partners to operate without creating continuity errors. Over the past decade, Chen digitized that information and then started watching movies, reading books, perusing video games, and the rest, all to make the database—the Holocron—as complete as possible. As of 2012, the Holocron contained "over 55,000 entries including over 19,000 characters, 2,900 species, 5,300 worlds, and 2,100 different types of vehicles," according to a blog post by Chen. He also created a team charged with making sure what was canonical remained consistent. This requires extraordinary attention to detail, as *Wired* pointed out:

Chen spends three-quarters of his typical workday consulting or updating the Holocron. He also approves packaging designs, scans novels for errors, and creates Talmudic charts and documents addressing such issues as which Jedi were still alive during the Clone Wars and how long it takes a spaceship to get from Dagobah, where Yoda trained Luke Skywalker, to Luke's homeworld of Tatooine. The Keeper of the Holocron takes this very seriously: "Someone has to be able to say, 'Luke Skywalker would not have that color of lightsaber.'"

When mistakes come up, Chen tries to resolve them or, when need be, make retroactive changes to maintain continuity. (There's even a term for this—"retcon.") However, that's not always possible.

Some of the early works are too complicated to fix retroactively—take the widely maligned Star Wars Holiday Special from 1978 or the first Star Wars novel, *Splinter of the Mind's Eye* (where Luke and Leia—siblings who don't know it yet—get a little frisky). Those are treated as outliers.

But the big category of outliers is flagged GWL. This is the stuff that drives hardcore Star Wars fans mad. For example, R2-D2 could fly in the prequels, but he forgot about that ability in the original trilogy. Both R2 and C3P0 served Obi-Wan Kenobi in the Anakin Skywalker stories, but in *A New Hope*, Obi-Wan had no knowledge of either of the droids, or vice versa. That stuff is all GWL. GWL is the only force more powerful than the Holocron.

GWL stands for George Walton Lucas.

BONUS FACT

You won't find the name of Yoda's species or its home planet in the Holocron. The former has never been named and the latter has never been identified.

DOUBLE BONUS!

In the summer of 2013, Star Wars debuted once more, and again in groundbreaking fashion. On July 3rd, *Star Wars Episode IV: A New Hope* became the first major motion picture to be translated and dubbed into Navajo, as part of an effort to keep the dying Native American language alive for another generation. As NPR reported, the Navajo version was screened at the Navajo Nation Fair in Window Rock, Arizona, and is now available on DVD.

TOY RESTORE-Y
WHEN BUZZ LIGHTYEAR ALMOST WENT BEYOND INFINITY AND RIGHT TO ZERO

In 1995, Pixar released the movie *Toy Story*, the tale of a room full of toys who—when real people aren't looking—turn out to be alive. Two of the toys—Woody, a cowboy, and Buzz Lightyear, an astronaut—lead the gang, both vying to be the favorite of a boy named Andy. They're joined by toy soldiers, a Slinky dog, and of course, Mr. Potato Head. The movie was a box-office smash, earning more than $360 million and warranting a sequel four years later. It too was a major success, earning another $485 million at the box office, leading to a third movie in the series. But the second film in the series almost never hit theaters, because Pixar almost accidentally deleted it.

You've probably been in the situation where something goes wrong with whatever technology you're using, and *poof!* your data is gone. Maybe you accidentally deleted a video off your phone. Perhaps you were writing a college paper and your computer crashed—without a backup. Maybe you were downloading a file and your connection timed out. Or maybe you dropped your device and it smashed, taking your photos with it. It's not hard to see how digital data can disappear despite our best efforts.

In most cases, though, major media companies don't have that problem. First of all, it's really hard to drop a huge set of servers into a toilet or onto the concrete, and second, things like massive crashes don't typically result in data deletion. But sometimes things go wrong, and in this case—for reasons unclear—a system administrator decided to run a special command (rm *, if you understand Unix commands) on one of Pixar's servers. That command quickly and thoroughly erased the drive.

Unfortunately, the drive contained a bunch of really important data for the movie—"databases containing the master copies of characters, sets, animation, etc.," according to a computer graphics developer who was working on the project. Galyn Susman, the movie's supervising technical director, claimed that the deleted work would have required "twenty or thirty people working for a solid year" to recreate what was lost. While this might be an exaggeration, the data loss was a big deal.

But, you say, they had their backup drives. After all, this was Pixar, a major media company. They have all sorts of redundant backup systems, right? Right! So, no problem.

Except that the backups had been failing for the last month, and no one knew. It turned out that the backups were spitting out error messages, but for some reason, the error messages were being repressed (likely due to a full disk) and therefore, no one was informed that something was wrong. The last two months of work on *Toy Story 2* was gone forever.

Until Susman realized that it had also gone somewhere else—it went home with her. She was, at the time, the mother of young children and wanted to be able to work from home. This was before the era of ubiquitous broadband, so she couldn't simply connect to the servers at the office. She had to make a copy of the files she needed, which in this case contained about 70 percent of what was lost. The team was able to recover almost all their work.

Ultimately, most of this wouldn't matter. After the incident, Pixar changed the script, and while many of the character and set models Susman and her team created were kept for the newer version of the movie, all the animations and most of the lighting went down the memory hole. The story of the near-disaster, though, did live on—a version of it is included as a bonus feature on the Blu-Ray version of *Toy Story 2*.

BONUS FACT

In *Toy Story*, Andy, the child who owns the toys, appears, as does his mother. But his father never does. Why? As one Pixar camera artist explained, "Human characters were just hideously expensive and difficult to do in those days and, as Lee mentioned, Andy's dad wasn't necessary for the story."

DOUBLE BONUS!

Toy Story and *Toy Story 2* may have saved an iconic toy from disappearing off shelves. Before the original movie in 1995, Ohio Art, the company that makes the Etch A Sketch, was in severe financial straits. After the Etch A Sketch made a twelve-second appearance in *Toy Story*, demand for the toy spiked. Sales fell off after a few more years, but in 1999, they spiked again. That second boost probably came from the toy's repeat performance—this time for forty-five seconds—in *Toy Story 2*.

RECOVERING NIXON
THE ONGOING EFFORTS TO UNERASE EIGHTEEN AND A HALF MINUTES OF HISTORY

As president, Richard Nixon wanted everything recorded for posterity—even the stuff he'd rather not anyone ever find out about. It ultimately led to his political downfall; as the Watergate scandal made headlines in 1973, the existence of his extensive recording system became public knowledge. Thousands of hours of conversations had been memorialized on tape, and there wasn't much anyone in the administration could do to prevent the public from finding out what secrets they held. But one tape is best known for what's missing—there's an eighteen-and-a-half-minute gap in the recording. Instead of words, there are clicks, buzzes, and static.

And it's treated like a national treasure.

Tape 342—that's what the archivist community calls it— contains this eighteen-plus minutes of erased information. However, because of its potential historical significance, we haven't given up hope yet of recovering whatever was said. The recording was originally made on July 20, 1972, three days after the break-in at the Watergate Hotel. Instead of conversation—most likely between Nixon and his then chief of staff, H.R. Haldeman—there's what appears to be static. No one knows what conversations were on those tapes—Nixon, if he knew and could remember, took that information to his grave—and the explanations for the erasures by the Nixon administration have fallen flat. In general, few scholars today assume that the erased portion of the tape contains explicit evidence of anything nefarious, but our natural human curiosity makes this mystery too juicy to ignore.

So we're not.

After Nixon left the White House, the National Archives and Record Administration (NARA) took possession of the tapes, including Tape 342. Today, it's stored in conditions that *Wired* magazine noted are typically reserved for documents and recordings that actually have comprehensible words contained within them:

> Stroll into the National Archives in College Park, Maryland, and ask to check out Tape 342, and the archivists will look at you as if you've asked to wipe your feet on the Declaration of Independence. Tape 342 is treated like a priceless heirloom, locked in a vault kept at precisely 65 degrees Fahrenheit and 40 percent relative humidity. The tape has been played just half a dozen times in the last three decades, and only then to make copies.

The reason? There's an ongoing hope that the information once recorded there will somehow be recovered. In August 2001, NARA began that rescue process in earnest, believing that advances in technology may be able to translate those buzzing noises into intelligible speech. The NARA experts began to make test tapes available to anyone with a theory as to how to translate the buzzes and noises into Nixon's words.

NARA didn't offer to pay anyone, but plenty of researchers took the bait—being the one to solve this mystery would be a reward in its own right (and probably lead to all sorts of new business opportunities). But about two years later, NARA again admitted defeat. Archivist John Carlin told the AP that he was "fully satisfied that we have explored all of the avenues to attempt to recover the sound on this tape" without success. But NARA wasn't giving up. He assured the press that NARA "will continue to preserve the tape in the hopes that later generations can try again to recover this vital piece of our history."

BONUS FACT

In 1960, Richard Nixon and John F. Kennedy faced off in the first-ever televised presidential debate. The debate appeared to go poorly for Nixon, who, unlike JFK, refused to wear makeup, an error amplified by the fact that he was suffering from flu-like symptoms and appeared very pale and lethargic. How much did this matter? According to History.com, a clear majority of those who watched the debate on TV thought JFK came out ahead. On the other hand, of those who listened on the radio, most thought that the result was a draw or that Nixon bested Kennedy.

CANCELING HISTORY
WHAT HAPPENS WHEN EVERYTHING YOU LEARN IN SCHOOL IS A LIE?

As May and June approach, children around the world are doing the same thing: studying or taking end-of-year exams. Here and there, some students are celebrating, because for some reason their exams were canceled. Maybe the photocopier broke? Or the teacher was sick that day? Maybe the power was out at school?

Or maybe everything they learned was a lie.

On May 31, 1988, that's what happened in the Soviet Union.

When Mikhail Gorbachev came to power in the 1980s, he ushered in a series of political reforms known as *glasnost*, or "openness," aiming to increase transparency concerning all the things in which the government was involved. Part of the process meant allowing for the critical re-examination of what the government had done in the past, and it quickly became clear that Gorbachev's predecessors had whitewashed most of this story. The stories and lessons included in a typical Soviet history education were incomplete at best and outright propaganda at worst. The *New York Times* quoted one student who said that her textbook had only one paragraph on Joseph Stalin, and not a very good one at that: "It said simply that he was a leader who had some problems."

So the nation needed to rewrite its history books.

But that decision was made late in the 1987–1988 school year and was not something the USSR could remedy overnight. The misunderstanding of history was pervasive across all sectors of life and had gone on for decades. As the *Los Angeles Times* reported, "even historians, social scientists and Communist Party theoreticians are uncertain what was correct, what was fantasy and what was a cover-up of crimes in the material taught Soviet students." The USSR's State Committee on Education hoped to have new textbooks ready in time for the following school year, but that seemed optimistic.

In any event, that wouldn't help with the more immediate problem. On the last day of May, roughly 53 million schoolchildren ages six to sixteen were scheduled for their end-of-year examinations. The government had just admitted that the history section of these exams was testing the students' knowledge of exaggerations, myths, and in some cases, outright lies. Gorbachev's government wanted to reverse this trend, so the officials took dramatic action. The government ordered that the exams be canceled—a move that the government-run newspaper *Izvestia* praised as a sign that *glasnost* was real: "Perhaps this, as nothing else, testifies to the triumph of new thinking, to the readiness to discard the traditional approaches. Only yesterday, one could not even suppose that such a decision was possible, let alone would be implemented."

But not all kids had reason to celebrate. Like many dramatic Communist orders, this one was controversial, hard to enforce, and therefore, easily ignored. As a result, many schools still administered exams in defiance of the edict—ironically, by testing their students on the now-admitted pseudo-history they had been taught over the past year.

BONUS FACT

In December 2012, a professor of computer science at Johns Hopkins University went to administer his final exam, only to find out that no one showed up. While he was probably surprised, he immediately understood why. He had previously announced (as he had since 2005) that he curved his exams so that the highest score was redefined to be a perfect grade. If everyone got a zero, then everyone's zero would be considered a 100 instead. His class rose to the occasion. They all boycotted the final and, in doing so, aced the test.

THE KALAMAZOO PROMISE
WHERE EVERYONE GOES TO COLLEGE FOR FREE

The city of Kalamazoo, Michigan, is the sixteenth most populous in the state, with just under 75,000 people according to the 2010 census. Like many Michigan municipalities, Kalamazoo's population has been shrinking over the past few decades; in 1990, it was home to more than 80,000 people. (Detroit, the largest city in the state, was at 1.027 million people in the 1990 census; per the 2010 census, Detroit's population is now just under 720,000.) In 2000, 24.3 percent of Kalamazoo's population was below the poverty line, including 26 percent—more than one out of four—of those age eighteen and under.

To help fix this, at the November 10, 2005, Kalamazoo Board of Education meeting, board members announced something dramatic: free or drastically reduced college tuition to many of the city's schoolchildren.

The program is called the "Kalamazoo Promise." Any student who attends the Kalamazoo public school system for at least four years and graduates receives a scholarship—including mandatory fees (but not room and board)—to any of Michigan's state colleges (and a dozen or so private colleges as well). The scholarship starts at

65 percent of one's costs and goes up 5 percent for each additional grade the child spends in the Kalamazoo school system. A child who goes to Kalamazoo's school system from kindergarten through twelfth grade, therefore, is eligible for 100 percent of his or her college tuition via the Promise. The Promise is backed by a group of anonymous donors, believed primarily to be comprised of members of the Stryker (of the Stryker Corporation) and Upjohn (of the Upjohn Company) families. There are rumors that former New York Yankee shortstop Derek Jeter (who grew up in Kalamazoo) is also involved.

The goals of the Promise are not just to encourage children to attend college (and to make that possible), but also to encourage families and businesses to relocate to Kalamazoo and keep a failing city moving forward. (In fact, the *New York Times* asserted that the Promise is "primarily meant to boost Kalamazoo's economy.") As of October 2010, almost five years after the Promise was announced, enrollment in Kalamazoo Public Schools was up 3 percent from the prior year, bucking the statewide trend. There are anecdotal reports of the school system improving and the real estate market rebounding; in the latter case, homeowners are regularly advertising their places as "Promise eligible," "Promise qualified," or the like, signifying that their home is in the geographic area covered by the Promise.

As of 2010, the Promise had paid out $18 million in tuition to roughly 2,000 high school graduates and shows no signs of stopping. The effect on students has been mixed, but shows—pardon the pun—promise. Kalamazoo is seeing measurable and positive results at the high school level, with jumps in college readiness rates that are markedly larger than statewide averages—and a reversal from the losses other urban centers in Michigan are experiencing. However, roughly half of those students who received scholarships (through 2011) dropped out of college before completing their program. The Promise's leadership is looking toward ways of better preparing eligible students for college.

BONUS FACT

Derek Jeter almost didn't play for the Yankees—he was almost drafted by another team, the Houston Astros. Jeter, fresh out of high school, was selected sixth overall in the 1992 Major League Baseball Draft by the Yankees. The Astros had the first pick but passed over him because they were concerned that he'd demand a higher-than-typical signing bonus. (Jeter had earned a baseball scholarship to the University of Michigan and could have used that as leverage.) Hal Newhouser, a Hall of Fame pitcher for the Detroit Tigers from the 1940s, was working for a scout for the Astros at the time and is credited with discovering Jeter. Newhouser forcefully advocated for selecting Jeter, but the Astros failed to take Newhouser's advice, selecting collegiate star Phil Nevin instead. Newhouser, enraged, quit.

INEMURI
REWARDED FOR SLEEPING AT YOUR DESK

It's fifth period biology class, maybe an hour after lunch. The professor is droning on about the Krebs cycle or something—you have no idea. While you're sitting upright with your eyes slightly open, you slowly drift off into a nap until your head falls forward, waking you suddenly. You look around, dazed, unsure of where you are or what just happened, but before anyone really notices (or lets on), you recover, barely, and are passably engaged with the class at hand.

This happens all too often—students, exhausted from class, homework, and the tensions of being teenagers, find themselves barely awake at their desks. So in 2006, a handful of high schools experimented with a straightforward approach—teachers encouraged students to take a brief after-lunch nap.

Not only that, but the high schools were actually behind the times. That's because they were in Japan, where sleeping at work is not only accepted but, at times, a sign of one's dedication and vigor. There's even a word for it—*inemuri*, which literally translates as "sleeping while present."

The theory is pretty straightforward: People who work hard get tired. On-the-job fatigue, therefore, is considered a sign of a productive employee. When you're tired, sometimes your body overrules your mind, and you fall asleep, even at work. While that's probably not acceptable in the United States and in other Western cultures, Japan is different—so different, that people will often take fake naps, just so their coworkers think that they've worked themselves to exhaustion. (One expert the BBC spoke with likened the practice to a UK worker sending an after-hours e-mail for the primary purpose of demonstrating that he or she is working well into the evening.)

Traditionally, only executives are permitted to practice *inemuri*, and when they do, they need to appear to be ready to wake at a moment's notice—sleeping upright, as if paying attention but for the fact that their eyes are closed. However, in recent years, these cultural restrictions have waned. Many retailers now sell desk pillows, explicitly marketed toward those who wish to take a snooze during the workday, and nap salons have emerged across the nation, charging the equivalent of a few dollars for a thirty-minute rental of a daybed within the confines of the spa. Some places also sell coffee designed to kick in with a jolt of caffeine twenty or so minutes after drinking—an office worker imbibes, naps, and is woken up by the drink in time to get back to work.

Most telling is how institutions are adopting the trend. It's not just schools such as the ones noted previously, nor are these small businesses. In 2006, the *Washington Post* reported that Toyota's offices (not dealerships) in Tokyo turned off the lights around lunchtime, and workers took fifteen- to thirty-minute power naps—with the approval of top brass. A company spokesperson told the *Post*, "When we see people napping during lunchtime, we think, 'They are getting ready to put 100 percent in during the afternoon.' Nobody frowns upon it. And no one hesitates to take one during lunchtime either."

BONUS FACT

At a young age, Bill Gates was recognized by his school's administrators for his prowess with computers (and not for good reasons—he and three friends had manipulated the computer lab's system to obtain extra computing time for themselves). The school asked Gates, still a student, to create a class scheduling system for them, and he agreed. He took advantage of it, though; as he'd later claim in a speech he'd give at his alma mater, "By the time I was done, I found that I had no classes at all on Fridays. And even better, there was a disproportionate number of interesting girls in all my classes."

WHAT ABOUT BOB?
HOW TO BE PRODUCTIVE AT WORK WITHOUT WORKING

In 2006, a report published by Inc.com concluded—ridiculously—that productivity losses cost U.S. employers more than half a trillion dollars—$544,000,000,000, to be a little more precise. The report found that in an eight-hour day, employees spent an average of 1.86 hours "on something other than their jobs, not including lunch and scheduled breaks." Of those surveyed, 52 percent "admitted that their biggest distraction during work hours [was] surfing the Internet for personal use."

The data is garbage, of course; the idea that employees should be always-on and that anything less is going to result in productivity losses isn't based in science or reality. But every once in a while, there's an example of an employee who goes to the extreme, not doing much work and perhaps none at all. Take, for example, a former software developer identified only as Bob. According to a report by NPR, Bob's schedule—determined by a retrospective look at his Internet browsing history—consisted of the following:

- 9:00 A.M.: Arrive and surf reddit for a couple of hours. Watch cat videos.

- 11:30 A.M.: Take lunch.
- 1:00 P.M.: eBay time.
- 2:00-ish P.M.: Facebook updates – LinkedIn.
- 4:30 P.M.: End-of-day update e-mail to management.
- 5:00 P.M.: Go home.

Curiously missing? Work. Apparently, Bob didn't do any.

That didn't match up with Bob's performance reviews, though. As TheNextWeb reported, Bob "apparently received excellent performance reviews, even being hailed the best developer in the building: his code was clean, well-written, and submitted in a timely fashion." He was, somehow, producing great work without actually working. Bob's employer didn't seem to notice that he wasn't doing any work, because from the corporation's vantage point, he was productive.

However, Bob's employer did notice something else—weird traffic coming into the company's servers through Bob's remote login credentials. The traffic seemed to be coming from China. To make matters even stranger, the Chinese connection via Bob's remote connection was active while Bob was sitting in the office. Baffled—why would Bob be logging in remotely from China while at his desk?—the company contacted Verizon, its telecom services provider.

The company assumed that some odd sort of malware had infected their systems, but that wasn't the case. Verizon determined that the problem was Bob himself—and it explained how a guy with great performance reviews matched up with that schedule of cat videos and shopping on eBay.

Bob had outsourced his work to China.

Verizon later determined that Bob had probably been doing this for a few years, using about a quarter of his pay to buy the services of lower-cost overseas providers. Bob was fired, of course—beyond the obvious fraud he committed, the employer was working on developing software for the U.S. government. Outsourcing that to China wasn't acceptable. But Bob probably laughed all the way to the bank. According to the Verizon security team, this wasn't his only job—and it probably wasn't the only job he had outsourced. Bob was making "several hundred thousand dollars a year," according to Verizon, and "only had to pay the Chinese consulting firm about fifty grand annually."

BONUS FACT

Give a customer service number a ring and there's a good chance your phone call will be connected to a representative stationed outside the United States. However, there's an increasingly decent chance you'll find someone in the United States on the other end of the phone. The reason? Many companies have found a low-cost, domestic solution: prison inmates. According to CIO.com, prisoners earn about $1 an hour to provide level-one support to customers in need.

THE CHIMERA
THE WOMAN WITH THE WRONG DNA

Embezzlement and on-the-job scams are pretty common—especially when compared to surrogacy scams. Typically, a surrogacy scam occurs when a female fraudster promises to carry a couple's fetus to term, but along the way pads the bill well beyond what one would have reasonably expected. Sometimes, it can get even worse.

And sometimes it's just a cruel trick of science.

Jamie Townsend and Lydia Fairchild were an unmarried couple who separated in 2002. When they split, Fairchild was pregnant with Townsend's child, and she requested government assistance in her home state of Washington. She claimed that she had two children, both from Townsend. Washington, to combat welfare fraud, required DNA tests from new applicants and their families—the state wanted to make sure that the children are actually those of the claimants—which Fairchild gladly agreed to provide.

But the DNA didn't match. According to the tests, the children Fairchild had been claiming were not her own. The authorities believed they had a more insidious scheme in front of them. They believed that Fairchild wasn't the children's actual mother but rather a surrogate—one who kept children for herself in order to collect welfare payments.

Fairchild protested, offering pictures of her two previous pregnancies, photos from the delivery room, and even the testimony of the delivering obstetrician. But those, the government argued, didn't matter. On the other hand, the DNA was dispositive. Fairchild, they concluded, was lying, which meant that the two children in her custody weren't hers—and her pregnancy . . . who knows? Thoughts of surrogacy fraud entered the picture. To prove it, the court ordered that an observer be present when Fairchild gave birth and that a DNA test occur in the first moment of the new baby's life.

Again, the DNA failed to match. Fairchild, it seemed, was somehow stealing eggs and, ultimately, children, all as part of some complicated con game. She was almost certain to spend untold years living in a prison cell—until her lawyers discovered the story of a Boston-area woman named Karen Keegan.

According to ABC News, Keegan needed a kidney transplant, and her family members—including her children—underwent tests to see if any of them could be a viable donor. Instead, doctors discovered that Keegan had different DNA than her children, a familiar story to Fairchild's attorneys. Keegan's doctors concluded that she had something called chimerism (from "chimera," a part-lion, part-snake, part-goat from Greek mythology), a rarity to say the least. ABC News explained: "In human biology, a chimera is an organism with at least two genetically distinct types of cells—or, in other words, someone meant to be a twin. But while in the mother's womb, two fertilized eggs fuse, becoming one fetus that carries two distinct genetic codes—two separate strands of DNA." In Keegan's case, a sample from a thyroid nodule contained the same DNA as her children, even though most of the rest of her did not.

There are only a few dozen documented cases of chimerism in humans worldwide, and it turns out that Fairchild was one of them.

Doctors administered a pap test, discovering DNA that matched her children. Fairchild had two different sets of DNA, explaining the previous mismatches.

She was deemed innocent of all charges levied against her.

BONUS FACT

If you want to tell two identical twins apart, a DNA test won't help, because they have the same DNA. What will help? Their belly buttons. Belly buttons are scars, as Wikipedia notes, and are not determined by genetics. (Fingerprints also work here—identical twins do not have identical fingerprints—but that's not as much fun.)

TWO BOYS NAMED JIM
THE COINCIDENCE THAT MAY BE DESTINY

As of February 8, 1979, James Arthur Springer—Jim, as he went by—had been twice married. His first marriage, to a woman named Linda, ended in divorce. His second wife was named Betty. Jim Springer grew up in Ohio and once owned a dog named Toy. He had a son named James Allan (although perhaps with one L). He was a chain-smoker who liked beer. In his garage he had a wood-working bench. He drove a Chevy, suffered from high blood pressure and migraines, and once served as a sheriff's deputy. His family lived on a quiet street—theirs was the only house on the block.

As of February 8, 1979, James Edward Lewis—Jim, as he went by—had been twice married. His first marriage, to a woman named Linda, ended in divorce. His second wife was named Betty. Jim Lewis grew up in Ohio and once owned a dog named Toy. He had a son named James Allan (although perhaps with one L). He was a chain-smoker who liked beer. In his garage he had a woodworking bench. He drove a Chevy, suffered from high blood pressure and migraines, and once served as a sheriff's deputy. His family lived on a quiet street—theirs was the only house on the block.

As of February 8, 1979, Jim Springer and Jim Lewis had almost no knowledge of one another. They had met before, but only as infants. On February 9, 1979, the two met for the first time in nearly forty years.

They were identical twins, given up for adoption as one-month-olds, now reunited.

The shocking coincidence seems like that of myth, but it's almost certainly not—shortly after the twins' reunion, *People* magazine and *Smithsonian* magazine reported on the incredible confluence of genetically identical twins with anecdotally identical lives.

The two men piqued the curiosity of a researcher named Thomas J. Bouchard, a professor of psychology and the director of the Minnesota Center for Twin and Adoption Research at the University of Minnesota. Bouchard studied their lives and similarities. Some of those parallel facts were purely coincidences—the two Jims' adoptive parents, who didn't share their DNA, named them both James. But Bouchard and his team concluded, as he stated in a research grant application, the evidence "continue[d] to suggest a very strong genetic influence on almost all medical and psychological traits."

Bouchard was able to secure funding to investigate the link between twins further and, over the course of decades, was able to study many pairs of identical twins who were raised apart from one another. He discovered many examples of twins who, each having no knowledge of the other, nevertheless made strikingly similar decisions (although none were as well known as Jim Springer and Jim Lewis). All together, Bouchard concluded that "shyness, political conservatism, dedication to hard work, orderliness, intimacy, extroversion, conformity, and a host of other social traits are largely heritable." That's not to say that we're slaves to our genetics—certainly not. However, they hold mysteries and relevancies that we are far from fully understanding.

BONUS FACT

Mark Twain wasn't a twin, but he often would tell people otherwise. According to the book *The Wit and Wisdom of Mark Twain*, the author would recount the tragic—but fictional!—tale of his brother Bill, who drowned in a bathtub . . . maybe. Mark (really Samuel Clemens) and Bill were so similar, no one—not even their mother—could tell them apart. So no one was sure which of the two had died. A terrible story to make up? Yes, but Twain let listeners off the hook with his punch line: He'd say that he was the one who drowned.

RICHARD PARKER
THE WORST NAME TO HAVE IF YOU REALLY LIKE THE WATER

Famed writer Edgar Allan Poe wrote seventy poems and sixty-six short stories during his forty years on this planet, but he published only one novel. That book, titled *The Narrative of Arthur Gordon Pym of Nantucket*, is fiction, focusing on Pym's misadventures as a stowaway on a whaling ship.

It also makes for a very interesting warning for those wishing to take to sea—if your name is Richard Parker, at least.

The novel, published in 1838, involves an attempted mutiny on the whaling ship. Pym and two others repel the mutineers, killing or throwing overboard all but one. The spared mutineer, named Richard Parker, is kept aboard in order to help operate the ship. This turns out to be inadequate, as the ship capsizes, leaving the quartet shipwrecked and without adequate food. Parker suggests that cannibalism is the only way out, and they draw straws to determine the victim. Parker loses and becomes dinner.

Again, that is fiction. But in 1846—just eight years after Poe published his novel—a real-life Richard Parker died in a shipwreck. He and twenty others were aboard the doomed *Francis Spaight*, which sank, killing all on board. This is, in and of itself, much ado about nothing; it is a mere coincidence and not a very good one at that, as it involves neither mutiny nor cannibalism.

But fast-forward a few decades to 1884, and the coincidence becomes downright creepy. A yacht named the *Mignonette* sank, and four people—just like in the story of Arthur Gordon Pym—made their way into a lifeboat. Just as in Pym's tale, the four found themselves lacking food and grew desperate. They did not draw straws, however; rather, two of the remaining three simply killed the youngest, a cabin boy who had fallen into a coma. All three then dined on the now-deceased seventeen-year-old. The cabin boy's name, of course, was Richard Parker.

As for mutiny, one needs to travel back in time to 1797, before Poe penned his novel—although there is little evidence that Poe had known about this incident. That year, another man named Richard Parker led a mutiny at the British naval base at Nore, commandeering a number of ships. As food began to run out, Parker ordered "his" fleet to head toward France. (Thankfully, there was no cannibalism this time.) The ship he was on followed this order but none of the other ships obeyed, and Parker was apprehended. He was hanged for treason.

This series of coincidences has not gone entirely unnoticed. In 2001, author Yann Martel published *The Life of Pi*, later made into a feature-length movie. It tells the story of a man who finds himself stranded on a lifeboat with a few animals, including a Bengal tiger. Martel paid homage to the shipwrecked men referred to previously by naming the tiger Richard Parker. While there is probably nothing to these coincidences, if your name is Richard Parker, you may want to stay away from boats.

BONUS FACT

The murder of Richard Parker on the *Mignonette* is famous for another reason—the later trial of Parker's murderers became a leading precedent in criminal common law jurisprudence. In the case, *Regina v. Dudley and Stephens*, the defendants argued that they committed the murder out of necessity, but the court ruled that necessity is no defense to murder. The case is now widely taught in law schools throughout the United States, but, if experience is any guide, few professors make reference to the coincidence of the victim's name.

THE TELLTALE TOASTER
THE MAN WHO KEPT COMING BACK

On October 3, 1849, a stranger found Edgar Allan Poe delirious (but, despite some reports, probably not drunk) and stumbling around the streets of Baltimore, Maryland. Poe—who was usually a very fashionable man—was wearing unkempt clothing, which fit poorly. His shoes were in dire need of a shine and repair, as the heels had been worn down significantly. Many believed he had been wearing someone else's attire, as his outfit didn't match his reputation. To make matters more interesting but even less clear, no one (publicly, at least) knew of Poe's whereabouts for almost a week before his discovery on the 3rd.

Unfortunately, we'll never know what happened. Poe died on October 7 and never recovered enough during the interim period to explain how he fell into such a state.

Yet, as strange as the circumstances around Poe's death may be, what happened to him generations later is probably stranger. For decades, every year on the same day each year, a costumed man visited Edgar Allan Poe's gravesite, leaving no explanation as to his motives or identity. Then, one year, he stopped, never to return.

The origins of the Poe Toaster, as the Baltimore press and community have dubbed him, are as mysterious as his motives. At some point in the 1930s—the exact year has been lost to history—the Poe Toaster arrived at the author's original gravesite (it was moved in 1875) on January 19, Poe's birthday. Every morning on that day, the Poe Toaster arrived wearing all black (including a wide-brimmed hat) except for a white scarf. A hood obscured the man's face, and he carried with him a silver-tipped cane. He'd pay his respects to the famous man once buried at that site, decorating the grave with three roses and an unfinished bottle of cognac and, at times, leaving a note.

These notes referred to the greatness of Poe, at least in the Toaster's eyes. But in 1993, the already strange gravesite ritual became downright cryptic; the note read, simply, "The torch will be passed." By then, the Toaster—assuming it was the same person the whole time—had been carrying out that ritual for sixty years, and some assumed that he was looking to retire (or had come to terms with his own mortality). This line of speculation became stronger in 1999, when the note referred to the sons of the Toaster. Further, that year, Toaster-watchers noticed that the man in black appeared younger than in previous years.

Thereafter, the notes seemed increasingly out of character for the Toaster. In 2001, the note referenced the upcoming Super Bowl versus the New York Giants and the hometown Ravens, but was markedly pro–New York. In 2004, the Toaster came to the grave during a short but notable anti-French period in the United States, due to France's unwillingness to join in military efforts in Iraq. (Remember "freedom fries"?) The Toaster's note apparently reflected this undercurrent of American sentiment (with poor grammar included): "The sacred memory of Poe and his final resting place is no place for French cognac. With great reluctance but for respect for family tradition the cognac is placed. The memory of Poe shall live evermore!"

In 2009—the 150th anniversary of Edgar Allan Poe's birth—the Poe Toaster made his final appearance. Through 2014, he has not appeared again at Poe's grave on January 19, although a handful of copycats (lacking the true Toaster's telltale habits) have come in his place. Jeff Jerome, a former curator of the Poe House and Museum who has collected the Toaster's notes over the years, declared in 2012 that the tradition had come to an end—with few remaining clues as to the Toaster's true identity.

BONUS FACT

The Baltimore Ravens are nicknamed for Edgar Allan Poe's famous poem, "The Raven." From the team's founding in 1996 through 2008, they had three mascots—all costumed performers dressed as ravens—named Edgar, Allan, and Poe. For the 2009 season, though, Edgar and Allan were retired and replaced with two live ravens named Rise and Conquer.

STICHTING DE EENZAME UITVAART
WHY YOU CAN'T DIE ALONE IN AMSTERDAM

Every year, countless numbers of people pass away alone, without family or friends to give them a proper funeral. In many places, the government and other organizations take care of the not-so-pleasant stuff like disposing of the person's stuff, figuring out what to do with the body, etc. We won't go into details, but let's just say that they get the stuff done that has to get done—but in a bureaucratic way.

However, just because someone dies alone doesn't mean that he or she should be buried unceremoniously. In Amsterdam, at least, such people aren't.

About twenty times a year, someone in Amsterdam dies without next of kin or somebody to claim the deceased's body. That might mean that these people would be buried without anyone noticing, but for roughly twenty-five years, a man named Ger Frits has made sure that doesn't happen. As reported by Radio Netherlands Worldwide in 2010, with the blessing and assistance of Amsterdam's city services Frits became a one-man funeral gathering. After the city agency notified him that someone had died leaving no one behind, Frits would go to the apartment of the recently deceased to get a feel for that person's life, desires, and interests. Then, based on the information he gathered, he'd select some music to play at the funeral—a ceremony only he'd be attending. He'd also bring flowers to leave at the gravesite.

For more than a decade, Frits did this all by himself. Then in 2002, a poet named Frank Starik asked if he could get involved. Starik believed that the recently passed deserve eulogies, even if they don't have friends, and he offered to compose poems for each. Frits appreciated the added dignity that Starik could bring, and suddenly, the two were partners in bringing solemnity to those who would otherwise meet a quiet, unnoticed end.

Today, the pair is known in Amsterdam as *Stichting De Eenzame Uitvaart*—the Lonely Funeral Foundation. They've started something of a movement. In other cities in the Netherlands and Belgium, volunteers are mimicking Frits and Starik's work, bringing music and poetry to those in their areas who died without friends or relatives.

BONUS FACT

In 2007, a forty-five-year-old Bosnian man named Amir Vehabovic died. His funeral only had one attendee—his mom. Normally this wouldn't be interesting—that stuff probably happens more than you'd think—except that Vehabovic wasn't really dead. He suspected that his friends didn't really like him, so he faked his own death (bought a fake death certificate, bribed the undertakers, procured an empty coffin) to see if they cared enough to send their last respects. They didn't.

INDEX